fallenstars

tragic lives & lost careers

by Julian Upton

critical vision — an imprint of headpress

A Critical Vision Book
Published in 2004
by Headpress

Headpress/Critical Vision
PO Box 26
Manchester
M26 1PQ
United Kingdom

[tel] +44 (0)161 796 1935
[fax] +44 (0)161 796 9703
[email] info.headpress@zen.co.uk
[web] www.headpress.com

British Library Cataloguing in Publication Data
A catalogue record for this book is available from the British Library

ISBN 1-900486-38-5

FALLEN STARS
Tragic Lives & Lost Careers
Text copyright © Julian Upton
This volume copyright © 2004
    Headpress
Layout & design: Walt Meaties & David
    Kerekes
World Rights Reserved

Front cover photos, clockwise from top left: Charles Hawtrey, Benny Hill, Diana Dors, Peter Sellers.

Back cover, from top: Dudley Moore & Peter Cooke (in Bedazzled), Ian Hendry (with Michael Caine in Get Carter), Terry-Thomas. Backdrop is Benny Hill.

Images are reproduced in this book as historical illustrations to the text, and grateful acknowledgement is made to the respective studios and distributors.

Contents

6   *Acknowledgements*
7   *Introduction*

1   Fame and Misfortune

9   Carol White   *Hollywood and Bust*
15   Rachel Roberts   *Paradise Lost*
23   Oliver Reed   *Hyde in Plain Sight*
32   Diana Dors   *The Lakes Regress*
39   Mary Millington   *True Blues*

2   Tragic Comics

48   Tony Hancock   *Down and Under*
53   Richard Beckinsale *The Dark Light Comedian*
56   Peter Sellers   *Curse of the Pink Panther*
66   Charles Hawtrey   *Sixteen Year Bender*
72   Benny Hill   *The Show's Over*
78   Terry-Thomas   *Temporarily Embarrassed*
84   Barry Evans   *Misadventures of a Taxi Driver*
90   Peter Cook   *A Life in Pieces*
97   Dudley Moore   *On the Rocks*

3   Final Acts

105   Mary Ure   *Anger and After*
109   Vivien Merchant   *Betrayal*
114   Jill Bennett   *Love and Death*
120   Ian Hendry   *The Nearly Man*
125   David Rappaport   *Even Dwarves Started Small*
129   Charlotte Coleman   *Forever Young*
133   Sir Stanley Baker   *The Outsider*

138   *Appendix: Selected Filmographies*
154   *Appendix: References*
156   *Index*

fallenstars

Acknowledgements

I'd like to convey my special thanks to David Kerekes, for supporting and guiding this book from its first tentative steps to the finished product, for his mentorship and professional assistance, and for his genuinely constructive (and mercifully minor) criticisms. To my mind, David is a bit like a benevolent Roger Corman, giving much-needed breaks to relatively untried talent, but without the pressure to make a fast buck or a cheap cash-in. Perhaps Critical Vision is the publishing equivalent of New World Cinema, albeit more intelligent and quality-driven.

Thanks also to Doug Jewsbury for help with the proofreading.

A version of the chapter, The Outsider, first appeared in *Planet*, Dec 2001.

In memory of Peter James Upton (1945–97)

Introduction

The brittle nature of film star fame and fortune, how easily it can shatter and fall through the fingers of those who are lucky enough to achieve it, is a subject that has fixated scandal-hungry film fans since the first decades of popular movie history.

Perhaps there is a certain relish to be had in 'seeing it all go wrong' for the rich and famous. Maybe there is a morbid symmetry to it, a kind of poetic justice. Certainly, such cautionary tales illuminate our own lives with an irresistible horror. From its earliest days, Hollywood has been littered with the bodies of performers whose careers were shattered, whose lives fell victim to drink, drugs and other misfortunes. *Fallen Stars* is fuelled by my own fascination with these tragic icons and soured dreams, and turns the focus onto British film and TV actors.

Not everyone in the chapters that follow can be easily pigeonholed as a 'fallen star', however. This is not intended, after all, as a collection of exclusively 'riches-to-rags' stories. Peter Sellers, Rachel Roberts and Oliver Reed, for example, were in high demand, and could still command heavy paychecks, at the time of their deaths. But their stories serve to illustrate that there are different ways in which talent can be squandered and in which lives can be abused.

'Fame and Misfortune' (Part One) deals with those who experienced great fame of a kind, only to abandon it — or find it abandoned — because of the demons lurking within them or forces beyond their control. These are the legacies tainted with stories of excess, indulgence and misunderstanding — the cracked actors, the washed-up sex symbols, the archetypal fallen stars.

Part Two looks at the tormented clowns — familiar entities since the days of silent film. Benny Hill, Dudley Moore, Peter Cook, Tony Hancock: all had their moments of comic genius. But in private they were troubled men, crippled by intense sadnesses. Richard Beckinsale, on the other hand, seemed healthy and happy in his personal and professional life. His, instead, is a story of a burgeoning, wildly successful comedy career cut short by circumstances outside his control. Nevertheless, there was a darker, more unfulfilled side to

Beckinsale, one that seems to fit the template of the melancholy comedian.

Part Three is where the forgotten or semi-forgotten actors lie. Among them, Ian Hendry, Mary Ure and Vivien Merchant. These performers never really found the recognition, or the enduring success, that they deserved. And, almost invariably, they fell into decline after only a brush with true acclaim. In many cases, this is all the more tragic, for 'Final Acts' charts how some of the most impressive British talent of stage and screen went to waste or dissolved in obscurity.

There is, arguably, a tabloid sensibility to *Fallen Stars*. But the book also hopes to revive interest in some of the lesser-known actors it features. It is, then, as much about forgotten careers and unfulfilled promise as it is about lives destroyed by booze, barbiturates or broken health. The pursuit of success — both personally and professionally, as these stories testify — can be as dangerous as it is enticing. And fame, of course, always comes at a price.

Part 1: Fame and Misfortune

Carol White

Hollywood and Bust

There is a disturbing scene in Michael Apted's terrific, and still underrated, 1977 thriller, *The Squeeze*, in which Carol White is forced to strip for her kidnappers. As they goad her, she weakly performs a time-honoured routine that rests uneasily between the coldly titillating and the heartbreakingly unerotic, and draws us guiltily into the dubious voyeurism of the whole sorry setup. And although the sordid mechanics of the strip are expertly manipulated by Apted, our discomfort is somehow exacerbated by the fact that Carol White is performing it. Thirty-four, losing her figure and already well into a steep career decline, the pain and humiliation she conveys in this scene betrays a jarring parallel with her real life.

What happened to White at the pinnacle of her career in the late sixties is not all that different from the demeaning fate that befalls her character in *The Squeeze*. Here was a precociously talented, beautiful British actress with some significant work behind her, 'kidnapped' by Hollywood, required to strip, and then discarded when her usefulness ran out. Although this analogy over-dramatises what essentially forms the sad career pattern of all too many actresses, the parallels are irresistible. One significant difference, however, is that Ms White was completely complicit in her glamorous kidnapping. The high life beckoned, and that was too big a draw for the working class girl from Hammersmith.

That an actress of Carol's instinctive talent decamped to Hollywood and to a slate of worthless films so quickly and so willingly was also indicative of a dichotomous outlook that ultimately contributed to her acting downfall. For all the raw investment in her best roles, White was never one to turn down the glitzy Cinderella treatment. She fell hook, line and sinker for the stretched limousines and sparkly dresses that Tinseltown had to offer, even if to embrace such excess would cost her her artistic credibility.

Indeed, she had displayed these traits very soon after her career took

Carol White

off, while still in Britain. Acting simultaneously in Ken Loach's characteristically downbeat *Poor Cow* (1967) and Michael Winner's frothy *I'll Never Forget What's'isname* (1967), White was subjected to the gritty immersion of the Loach set one day and the champagne guzzling of the Winner set the next. And it was clear which lifestyle she preferred. But who can blame her for that?

Yet it was with Loach, with his skill for evoking powerful naturalism, that Carol White gave her best performances. And, ironically, it was with Loach — socialist filmmaker and thorn in the side of the establishment — that she became a genuine star. Loach's *Cathy Come Home* (1966) is a milestone of British television history, perhaps more politically significant than anything ever seen at the UK cinema. A searing, documentary-style account of the plight of a homeless woman and her children, its impact was so profound that it is still regarded today as a yardstick for quality, issue-led drama in Britain. That it was seen by so many people (a quarter of the population) is of course a testament to the power of television. That it was so authentic, absorbing and heartbreakingly real was down to Loach's uncompromising vision and White's primal performance.

Some of Carol's scenes in *Cathy Come Home* appeared so authentic as to be, at the time, almost unbearable to watch. Certainly, nothing like it had been seen on British television before. Carol's own children, Sean and Steve, were cast as her children in the TV film, adding a further emotional depth to the production. Famously, the impact of the programme led to the establishment of the homeless charity Shelter. It also brought Carol White to true prominence after ten years in the business.

White had performed as a juvenile actor since 1956. She had been busy with walk-ons since that time, and appeared more notably in *Carry on Teacher* (1959), *Beat Girl* (1960), *Linda* (1960) and the gritty drama *Never Let Go* (1960), chiefly memorable for Peter Sellers' straight turn as a villain. She took some time out to marry the musician Mike King and have children, and then returned to acting, but it wasn't until 1965, and another gritty TV play, that she was first really noticed. As a factory worker who chooses to have an abortion in Nell Dunn's drama *Up the Junction* (always jolly, these BBC TV plays), White so impressed the writer Jeremy Sandford that he wrote *Cathy Come Home* with her specifically in mind.

Three years later, with Loach's *Poor Cow* attracting good reviews and *I'll Never Forget What's'isname* grabbing attention for different reasons (it was the first mainstream film in which the word 'fuck' was uttered), Carol found herself being wooed by Hollywood. The producer Irv Levin of National General offered her $150,000 to appear in a US thriller, *Daddy's Gone A-Hunting*, with the promise of two movies to follow. At the same time, Ken Russell offered her a part in *Women in Love* for £10,000. Turning her back firmly on DH Lawrence and the challenges of a brooding classic, White accepted Levin's proposal (as well as his bed for the night) and decamped to LA in 1968. Immediately she was showered with riches, attention, parties and the amorous advances of famous and powerful men. And although she lapped it up, fourteen years later she opined that going there "was the biggest mistake of my whole life".

Certainly, from the perspective of her career, things did start to go wrong in Hollywood almost immediately. *Daddy's Gone A-Hunting* (1969) was a formula thriller that did not perform to expectations, despite the permissive-era helping of a semi-nude Carol that it served up. Worse, Irv Levin's wife found out about his brief tryst with Carol and tried to commit suicide. In the meantime, Carol had put the final nail in the coffin of her marriage to Mike King by having a much-talked-about affair with her co-star in the film, another married man, Paul Burke. Clearly, National General balked at Carol's reckless dallying with married men. Citing her unscheduled trip back to London to visit her ill father as breach of contract, the studio cancelled her three-picture deal, retrieved the blue Mercedes that Levin had given her and offered her next film, *The Grasshopper* (1969), to Jacqueline Bisset.

Despite these setbacks, Carol won roles in other Hollywood films. But these all turned out to be as disappointing as *Daddy's Gone A-Hunting*. Typical cheesecake parts, they required only a pretty face, pert breasts,

Das faszinierende Tagebuch einer jungen Frau

Carol White
Terence Stamp
in
POOR COW
Geküsst und geschlagen
Regie : Kenneth Loach
Ein Farbfilm von Nell Dunn und Kenneth Loach
nach dem Roman "Poor Cow" von Nell Dunn
Musik und Gesang:
Donovan
Eine Joseph Janni
Produktion der
Vic-Films, London

White with co-star Paul Burke. ***Daddy's Gone A-Hunting***

and the promise of sexual relief for has-been heroes like Dean Martin and Rod Taylor.

Unstimulated by these flat experiences, Carol began to seek out other pleasures to fill the pockets of emptiness and boredom that stretched end-lessly through the process of Hollywood film-making — namely, drinking, spending and drug-taking. She was still earning more than she ever could back home — since she'd been in LA she'd earned and spent a million dollars — and was by now partying with the likes of Frank Sinatra and James Caan. But she was permanently shrouded by an unforgiving streak of insecurity and low self esteem, a trait that had its origin in an incident of sexual abuse that had occurred in her childhood. And she was especially troubled by the continued turbulence of her affair with Paul Burke (the final straw was when he rang her up to wish her Happy New Year and inform her that he was in bed with two hookers). In January 1970, Carol attempted suicide by downing a bottle of pills and "the best part of a quart of vodka".

Back in London, she recovered, but not without some lasting emotional and psychological damage, which was no doubt exacerbated by the six courses of electric shock therapy that was required to bring her back to 'sanity'. Nevertheless, she resumed her career, and made *Dulcima* (1971) with John Mills, her most interesting film for several years. Remaining in London, she was soon back to her old ways, drinking champagne and cavorting with the likes of Oliver Reed and Warren Beatty (who regularly visited her after his girlfriend, Julie Christie, had gone off to work.)

In 1972, Carol walked off a Canadian-set action movie to make *Made* for producer Joe Janni. A self-conscious attempt to reprise the artistic integrity and commercial success of *Poor Cow*, *Made* was a gritty, downbeat study of an impoverished single mother. It was not without impact, but it singularly failed to reward anyone concerned. Still artistically unfulfilled and emotionally fragile, Carol White returned to Paul Burke in the States, whereupon she attempted suicide for the second time.

It is a poignant measure of just how needy for love and attention Carol White was that she fell in love with, and married, the psychiatrist who was by her bedside when she woke up from this second overdose. Dr Stuart Lerner was only twenty-three, but already a distinguished medical professional. He could have been a calming influence and a solid rock of emotional stability for Carol. But she soon tired of him. She missed the hard drinking, playboy volatility of Burke, and instead of calming down, she grew increasingly paranoid and hysterical during her years with Lerner, accusing him of mind control games and psychological manipulation. She made another film in Hollywood, the sexed-up curio *Some Call It Loving* (1973) — again interesting, again a flop — before beginning to turn down roles in the search for something of quality.

Her marriage to Lerner waning, Carol began to use cocaine heavily. In her autobiography, she described her typical drug diet in the mid seventies:

"I tried cocaine and I liked it. I didn't think I would get hooked, but every day I wanted more. On some days I had got so high I had to take Valium to bring me back down to earth. I took diet pills to lose weight, the result of a drinking spree that started on my wedding day; I took Quaaludes to relax and sleeping pills to block out everything."

When she was in London filming *The Squeeze* in 1976, her ex-husband noticed that her lifestyle was again taking Carol to dangerous places. In a 1992 *Sunday Times* article (by Peter Gillman) Mike King recounts visiting her and their sons in a rented Mews near Baker Street. King dropped in to find Carol sitting half-crazed, rocking back and forth and moaning "I want to die." She was grinding broken glass into her wrists. Only "a megadose of Valium and a hard slap in the face" brought her out of it.

Despite winning acclaim for her performance in *The Squeeze*, Carol's career went into further decline in the late seventies. She finally split with Lerner and shacked up with Mike Arnold, described by her ghost writer Clifford Thurlow as a "violent would-be hockey star, pop star, any kind of star". Arnold, a hulking, volatile builder, was sixteen years Carol's junior, and just her kind of man. He also turned out, according to Carol's son Steve, to have a penchant for domestic brutality, but Carol seemed perversely excited by this and often provoked him into his violent responses. Arnold came to dominate how Carol managed her career, or lack of it. Consequently, by the end of the seventies, she'd had little work outside a couple of episodes of the TV sitcom *Diff'rent Strokes*. Clifford Thurlow remembers, however, that at that time "Carol was an optimist. She was living in a rented flat with a shared pool.

As we sat each day under the palms sipping booze, men in brown overalls appeared and carried out the items in the flat: chairs, sofas, the bed, wine glasses, tropical sunsets in oil. Everything went over six months, except the telephone — lifeline of LA. Husband Mike chipped in by tarring roofs in the valley."

However, it was her involvement with Thurlow, and his supportive co-ordination of her hazy memories, that secured Carol's British 'comeback' in the early eighties. Selling a kiss-and-tell story to the *Sunday Mirror* and publishing her autobiography *Carol Comes Home* reminded British produc-ers that she was still around, still foxy. Simultaneously, she was offered a leading role in Nell Dunn's controversial West End play *Steaming* and a part alongside Joan Collins in the soft-focus sex film *Nutcracker* (1982).

Her command of the stage in *Steaming* was a triumphant return to form for the star whose beauty had all too often (of late) masked a true acting ability. Thurlow remembers her performance in the play as being electrify-ing, a sentiment that was echoed in the critical acclaim it received. Carol was immediately celebrated for getting through the sixties and seventies and 'coming home'; in her own words, she was 'a star who survived to tell the tale'. But the comeback lasted all of five minutes.

As she began work on *Nutcracker* (filming in the day and then performing *Steaming* at night), she was seduced again by the film star treatment she was receiving. And she needed the money. But the stage and film roles were hard to reconcile. Carol began missing performances of *Steaming*, and was subsequently fired. She completed *Nutcracker* and returned to the States. Somewhat predictably, *Nutcracker* — tepid sub-porn of the hokiest kind — duly bombed.

Back in Hollywood, Carol was fast approaching forty, and now found roles harder than ever to come by. Her brief triumph in London meant nothing to the executives in LA. Nevertheless, she cut down on the booze and the drugs and tried to apply herself. In 1984 she even freed herself of the burden of Mike Arnold. But it was to no avail. The smattering of parts she secured in the next few years were little more than walk-ons, undignified character parts in straight-to-video stinkers.

In the mid eighties Carol met Sue Robbins, an aspiring screenwriter who, somewhat unexpectedly, became the actress's partner. Robbins took the fall-ing star under her wing and provided for her as she became less employable and more addicted to drink and drugs. The two attempted to mount a horror film together, but nothing came of it. By the late eighties, Carol was reduced to calling her brother in London to borrow the occasional £500. Inevitably, she was becoming bitter and resentful, and could only block out the regret and the anguish with booze and cocaine.

At the start of the nineties, Carol followed Sue Robbins to Miami, where they holed up in a sparsely furnished hotel room and began to live a simpler life, away from the pressure to succeed that LA demanded of everyone. But Carol's drinking was worsening. Her appearance was ravaged, her stomach distended from the booze. By July 1991 she was regularly coughing up blood in the mornings. Doctors told her to stop drinking, but by this point she was unable to. The following month, her son Steve, who had come to stay with his mother and Robbins, woke in the hotel room to find Carol vomiting blood "by the bucketful". She was suffering from a massively ruptured oesophagus, a result of cirrhosis of the liver. Rushed to hospital, Carol lived on for another month but never regained consciousness. She died in hospital, aged forty-eight, on September 16, 1991.

It had been Carol's wish to be buried alongside her parents in London. But her sons and her friend Sue Robbins could not afford the $8000 that was needed to fly her body home. Peter Gillman, profiling Carol posthumously in the *Sunday Times*, reported that the last brutal irony of her tragic death was the manner in which she was returned to the UK. Her body was cremated at the Miami hospital in which she'd died and her cash-strapped sons had to mail her ashes to Britain. When 'Cathy' finally came home, it was in a brown paper parcel.

[*Carol White filmography p.138*]

Rachel Roberts

Paradise Lost

Rachel Roberts sprang from the dour confines of a South Wales valley in the twenties and spent her formative acting years, impoverished but enlightened, in rep. No great looker but intensely talented, these modest beginnings seemed to set her on course for a credible career on the British stage. But by the time of her early death, the trajectory of her life and career had gone off at some extreme tangents. By the mid-sixties, Rachel's small triumphs in the theatre and on the screen were being overshadowed by her jet-setting, sun-bathing, social-climbing life as the wife of a Hollywood superstar.

When Rachel married Rex Harrison in 1962, she became what she had always really wanted to be — a princess, rich and famous, romanced in a fairy tale travelogue that stopped off in New York, Paris and the Italian Riviera. For the rest of the decade, she shared the life of a man, who, in the autumn of his career, had secured his legend and was basking in a lifestyle of glitzy parties, exotic location filming, champagne by the pool and exhilarating drives in the soft-top. But when Rex left, the actress found herself trapped in a long, continuous fall.

Rachel's best work on film came early in her screen career, although she was already a mature, experienced actress by that time. At thirty-three, in the ground-breaking *Saturday Night and Sunday Morning* (1960), she oozed

Rachel Roberts

domestic sexuality as a bored, repressed housewife — all loose camisoles and tousled hair — passionately locked in a dangerous affair with Albert Finney, a wayward rogue ten years her junior. In that film, she spilled out of her nightie and onto our laps with an earthy charge that took the sink out of the kitchen and placed it firmly in the bedroom. She brought to the screen a new level of provincial eroticism. Although she wasn't pretty, Rachel Roberts could nevertheless smoulder with mousy Welsh magnetism, and what she lacked in looks she made up for with instinctive, intelligent talent. Three years on, she was foregrounded by Lindsay Anderson in his exceptional *This Sporting Life* (1963), and for this won even greater acclaim.

Rachel had met Rex Harrison, twenty years her senior, in 1960, when they both performed in Chekhov's *Platonov* at the Royal Court Theatre in London. For Rex, Hollywood's foremost light comedian, it was a therapeutic — and challenging — professional gear-change. He was still recovering from the tragedy of his last marriage (he had wed actress Kay Kendall knowing that she was dying from myeloid leukaemia, something he and the doctors kept secret from Kay herself; she died at thirty-three in 1959). For Rachel, it was another in a series of effortlessly intense stage performances. Rex was impressed by his co-star's talent and versatility; Rachel was taken by the raffish ease with which Rex carried off the lifestyle of a Hollywood Royal. They began a love affair, which Rachel, as she grew older — and sicker — came to reflect upon as a period of almost unbearable happiness.

Although coloured by sensual passion, fogged by chronic alcoholism and peppered with romantic fantasy, Rachel's strikingly well-written journals portray her relationship with Rex, in its early days at least, as a glittering fairy tale of the old fashioned kind. Writing in the last, troubled year of her life, she wistfully recalled how a girl like her would swoon for a man like Rex, and how "such a girl would grab at that worldly, sophisticated man who drank black velvets, listened to Ray Charles records, lived in Eaton Square, ordered chauffeur-driven cars, consumed her little body, praised her green eyes..." She went on: "We were together all the time. Ease entered my life. Rex took all the decisions. I had nothing to do but live for him. ... I prayed that the happiness would last."

Sadly, it didn't. Rachel, in keeping with her somewhat child-like view of romance and marriage (albeit one that was occasionally tainted by the exhibitionistic promiscuity of an 'artistic temperament') soon pretty much gave up her own career to follow Rex around the globe. In the wake of the Oscar-laden film version of *My Fair Lady* (1964), Rex was a superstar again, and was greeted with adoration wherever he stepped off the plane. High profile film offers continued to come his way, but Rachel, with such a promising film career in front of her, now took almost no work.

But like Rex, Rachel was a volatile, highly-strung character, and being known by the world's press simply as 'the fourth Mrs Rex Harrison' was damaging to her. And by devoting herself so completely to the life of one man, she left herself vulnerable to attacks of loneliness and perceived worthlessness when he wasn't around or when they argued, which, given their equally fiery temperaments, they often did.

One such occasion, in July 1965, saw Rachel washing down a handful of Seconal with mouthfuls of brandy after a particularly stormy evening with Rex. Rex arrived home in time to rush her to hospital, and she made a full recovery, and although the whole incident was probably more to do with attention-seeking than depression, it was a chilling portent of Rachel's approach to coping with unpleasant situations. It must have also been particularly alarming for Harrison, who had not only lost one wife to illness, but had also, famously, in 1948, had a lover (actress Carole Landis) commit suicide rather than be without him.

As the months of the marriage wore on, it was clear that Rachel's artistic confinement as Mrs Rex Harrison was steering her towards antisocial behaviour. She began drinking more heavily and took to making a fool of herself at parties and gatherings. To Rex, she again began to threaten to kill herself. Such desperation, although self-pitying, was understandable. Rachel was a driven actress, and naturally gifted — there was hardly a role she couldn't turn her hand to. She had prepared for performances with a mixture of sensitivity, perception, intuition and conscientious commitment. Although she was devoted to Rex, she now seemed little more than an exotic, caged bird. So Rex, who had been happy for his wife to stay 'at home', decided, for her sanity's sake, to encourage her to go back to work.

As a result, the couple appeared together in *A Flea in Her Ear* (1968), which was not a professional high point but at least made it known that Rachel was available again. But the failure of the released film, ultimately, did not

Rachel Roberts with Richard Harris.
This Sporting Life

do the Harrison marriage any favours. Rex's *My Fair Lady* honeymoon period was now at an end. The previous year's *Dr. Dolittle* (1967) had kept him visible, although as a musical it was clearly a second-rate affair in comparison with *Lady*. His next film, *Staircase* (1968), in which he and Richard Burton played homosexual hairdressers, was something of an unqualified disaster, however. More significantly, Rex was now growing bored with life with Rachel. And Rachel, although working again, was keeping her depression at bay with drink and drugs. By 1969, the marriage was clearly over, even if Rachel did not want to believe it.

When Rachel and Rex formally separated at Christmastime that year, Rachel made another suicide attempt, swallowing fifty aspirin. She spent Christmas Eve having her stomach pumped at St George's Hospital in London. Again, she appeared to make a robust recovery, but now seemed deluded about the state of her relationship with Rex. Some days earlier, she had said to a journalist: "The sixties are over and the seventies are here — let's all be friends. That's what Rex would want. I will see him soon. Ask me what I want for 1970 and I will say Rex." But Rex did not return the sentiment and the couple remained separated. Finally, in 1971, they divorced.

By now Rachel was forty-four, and childless. But she had not grown up. While remaining the epitome of the professional on stage and on screen (she scored another personal triumph, reunited with Albert Finney, as a bitter housewife in *Alpha Beta* at the Royal Court in 1972, a performance that was later filmed for cinema release), her behaviour outside of work was growing increasingly alarming. In the depths of her estrangement from Rex, she became more reliant on drugs and more unstable when drinking in company.

She behaved particularly outrageously while taping an episode of a BBC TV chat show with the affable Russell Harty, before a live audience, in early 1973. After a few moments of inconsequential chat, Rachel suddenly appeared extremely drunk and began talking of Rex Harrison. She then called Harty 'a silly cunt' and began laying into feminists, announcing, without much delicacy, that "all they need is a cock up their cunt or their arse." She followed this by turning to the gobsmacked family audience and informing them that all her cats wanted to do was screw. Before she was dragged off the stage, she was halfway through an impromptu rendition of The Lady Is A Tramp. Unsurprisingly, the show was never broadcast.

Yet she continued to hold it together as a serious actress. With a deep sense of discipline ingrained from her hard upbringing, Rachel was fearful of forgetting lines or letting her peers down, and she was still able to focus on her work. 1974 saw her delivering icily effective support in Sidney Lumet's star-studded *Murder on the Orient Express*, and landing Tony nominations for not one but two standout Broadway performances, in *The Visit* and *Chemin de Fer*.

But such artistic clear-headedness was not to last. Critical praise for her stage roles was not opening the door to happiness or any sense of security for Rachel. Even finding a caring, sensitive lover in Darren Ramirez, a Beverly Hills designer and hairdresser, had not settled her. In 1976, in what might be one of the most bizarre career moves of any actor, Rachel, the toast of New York theatre, signed up for a supporting role as a housekeeper in a lukewarm US sitcom, *The Tony Randall Show*.

After its first year, it was clear to everyone that *The Tony Randall Show* was not changing the face of television comedy, and there were few tears shed when it was dropped by its producing network, ABC. And this wasn't such a bad thing for Rachel, who'd done it for the experience and, if she put her mind to it, could return to more demanding roles. But then CBS picked up the series, and she found herself committed for another year.

The series' second season was an unhealthy one for Rachel. She was marginalised by the scripts and grew resentful of her involvement. But at least she still managed to separate her drinking from her work.

After *The Tony Randall Show* ended in 1977, Rachel drifted from the occasional decent screen role (in playwright Alan Bennett's *The Old Crowd* for British TV and *Yanks* [1979], directed by John Schlesinger) to such incongruous fare as the Chevy Chase/Goldie Hawn vehicle *Foul Play* (1978). For someone so accomplished, she was resolutely unpretentious in her career path. But she was facing another trial in her life, and one that signalled her final slide into helplessness.

In 1977 Rachel had turned fifty, and passing this milestone exacerbated her emotional fragility. Now she was not only childless, she also knew she would never be a mother. She surveyed, with heartbreaking envy, all her female friends with husbands and families around them. And more than ever, the subject of Rex Harrison began to dominate her thinking and her conversation. She began keeping a journal almost daily, only for it to dissolve constantly into laments about Rex and missed opportunities, and to express fear for the future. Her neuroses started to amplify. Her drinking, in between bouts of AA meetings, began to reach uncontrollable levels. And her thoughts turned frequently to suicide. Professionally, she was still able to sleepwalk through dross such as *The Hostage Tower* (1980), but her confidence as an actress was the next thing to be hit.

Symptomatic of her unpredictability and her constant desire for stimulation, Rachel, very unexpectedly, accepted a drama lecturing position at Yale University in early 1980. The delighted Dean immediately involved her in the development of a play by Athol Fugard, the college's writer-in-residence. The idea was that Rachel would lecture students and appear in the play, *A Lesson from Aloes*, and take it from its premier at Yale and on to Broadway.

But Yale was clearly a mistake from the word go. Its sombre, autumnal seriousness and disciplined devotion to academic achievement was anathema to a volatile thrill-seeker like Rachel. And the play she began to rehearse struck a disturbing chord with the actress. The role of an ageing South African housewife, prone to bouts of mental illness and traumatised by the country's oppressive regime, seemed to mirror metaphorically the very fears that dominated Rachel's private thinking.

The actress filled her free time in the leafy confines of Yale by drinking constantly. She latched onto Fugard and his family for company and support, but their patience did not really help her. (Fugard has said that, when putting her to bed one night after another bout of binge drinking, he found a bottle of sleeping pills and flushed them down the toilet. "A suicide at Yale would have been just unthinkable," he commented.) Rachel was becoming more obsessed with Rex Harrison, and more fearful of the torment that the role in the upcoming play would unleash within her. Soon after, Rachel withdrew from *A Lesson from Aloes*, the first time that she had abandoned a role. She also left Yale, and did not go back.

Still eager to work, however — perhaps pathologically dependent on it — Rachel secured a role, in April 1980, in what was to be, pitifully, her final film: *Charlie Chan and the Curse of the Dragon Queen*. Although the great Peter Ustinov was playing the eponymous detective, the title pretty much indicates all there is to say about the quality of the film. Even so, Rachel nearly lost that job, when, the night before rehearsals were to begin, she took another overdose. As

The Journals of
RACHEL ROBERTS
NO BELLS
ON
SUNDAY
EDITED AND WITH A DOCUMENTARY
BIOGRAPHY BY **ALEXANDER WALKER**

*'Everyone has not
only a story,
but a scream'*

Rachel Roberts with
Rex Harrison.
A Flea in Her Ear

she was being revived in hospital once more, her partner Darren convinced the film's director that she'd had an extreme reaction to something she ate and would be fine in a short while. After a few edgy days, Rachel did turn up for filming.

Once again, Rachel managed to convince many of her screen colleagues that she was nothing less than a gregarious Welsh girl without a care in the world. But some more astute observers, such as Ustinov, saw through this act. "I remember thinking she was a lady with some deep social problem — drinking, I thought — though she never let it show on the set," said the actor. "She was a little too over-cheerful for comfort, though. All her conversation came back to one topic — Rex, Rex, Rex."

Ustinov's observations were confirmed by Rachel's further decline after finishing work on *Charlie Chan*. From that point, her life became a series of hospital admissions, drying out treatments, embarrassing interludes and catastrophic depressions. Flitting between LA and London, in between hospital stays, she was cared for by concerned friends (of whom she had many), but the patience and stability they offered was often a double-edged sword for the star. More often than not, the peaceful domestic surroundings she found herself in brought home a lonely agony for Rachel. Seeing women of her own age flutter around their grown-up children and enjoy settled lives with their husbands was eventually too much for Rachel to bear.

In November 1980, the play that Rachel had found herself unable to perform, *A Lesson from Aloes*, opened on Broadway to rave reviews. Although still available for work, Rachel herself was now spending most of her time fastidiously keeping her journal, recording her torment and offering dark portents of a looming suicide.

The last entry in her diary was November 25, 1980. "I'm paralysed," she wrote. "What has happened to me? ... Day after day and night after night, I'm in this shaking fear. What am I so terribly frightened of? Life itself, I think."

The next day, Rachel's gardener found the fifty-three-year-old actress lying dead on the kitchen floor of the Los Angeles house she shared with Darren Ramirez. She had smashed into a glass screen used to divide the kitchen from the dining den, and there were sharp rips in her negligee and deep scratches in her bare legs. The gardener noticed that the kettle was still boiling.

Rachel's death was reported first as a heart attack, but the coroner later reported that she "died from swallowing a caustic substance", although it could not be determined whether it had been swallowed intentionally. The substance was described as a "lye, alkali or some deadly acid". Several days later, after also quantifying a large amount of barbiturates in Rachel's body, the coroner officially recorded a verdict of suicide.

Nevertheless, the presence of a 'caustic' substance in Rachel's body and the bizarre spectacle of her death scene — shattered glass and a boiling kettle — left many perplexed as to the true nature of her demise. Those who knew her well, however, were unsurprised by the verdict of suicide.

Her closest friends offered a number of conclusions that suggested that Rachel had planned a 'beautiful suicide'. A blanket had been found on the hill behind the house, where Rachel had loved to sit. Rachel, according to one theory, went there to die, swallowing handfuls of pills and lying under a wild-rose bush. Her friend Sybil Christopher concluded that "after swallowing the Nembutals and Mogadons … she found she wasn't 'going under' fast enough… I assume she felt chilly and, paradoxically, for someone intent on dying, staggered down the little steep flight of hillside steps to get another blanket … In her drugged state, she probably stumbled in and out of the rose bushes on the way down, which accounts for all the rips and snags in the nightie she was wearing."

Once in the house, Rachel started to eat a muffin. Unusual, but Darren Ramirez points to the advice given by the suicide counselling group Exit, whose pamphlets Rachel had recently read. "Suicide attempts are often frustrated because the person vomits up the pills. To avoid this, you should eat something solid."

The fact that the kettle was boiling was less explicable, but Sybil Christopher offered the theory that Rachel had done as she had always done, and "being British" put the kettle on "whenever she went into anyone's kitchen". It seems odd, to say the least, that she would have the presence of mind to put the kettle on in the middle of a suicide attempt, but Rachel could hardly be accused of acting rationally even at the best of times.

The presence of the caustic substance is something of a complete mystery, however. Alexander Walker, editing Rachel's journals, points out that "the substance is the basis of common household disinfectant: it is also used by some people as an insecticide or weedkiller. But no bottle so labelled was ever found." He goes on to suggest that Rachel may have secreted it away before, or found it outside, or drank it from a bottle assuming it was wine. Whatever happened, she did drink it. Again, her friends were forced to speculate that she did it to finish herself off properly when she thought the drugs weren't working.

Another thing open to speculation is whether Rachel had read that day's

Los Angeles Times. She had certainly seen it, given that a scribbled note in her handwriting on a copy was later found in her house. Inside the paper was an eye-catching report on the latest touring production of *My Fair Lady*, which had just reached San Francisco. The piece ended with a short, upbeat interview with the show's seventy-two-year-old star: the incomparable Rex Harrison.

The mystery of the exact circumstances of her suicide remains, but there is no doubt as to the desperate state of Rachel Roberts' mind at this time. And seeing an article about her beloved Rex, who was once more leaping into the limelight, as healthy and as magnetic as ever (and with another new wife waiting for him at home), could clearly have propelled her into putting an end to her suffering there and then.

Rex and Rachel had stayed friends after their split. Despite her increasing emotional instability, Rex had tried to steady her whenever he could. Ironically, when her body was discovered, he had been only a mile away, staying at the house of his friend, Leslie Bricusse. Two days later, Rex opened in *My Fair Lady* in San Francisco, in the shadow of the news that yet another actress who'd been romantically linked to him had met an untimely demise. The show, of course, had to go on.

[*Rachel Roberts filmography p.139*]

Oliver Reed

Hyde in Plain Sight

In Britain in the mid nineties, a reaction against political correctness — which, often in its most naïve, fundamental and humourless form, had been dominating a great deal of popular culture for ten years or more — had its mainstream beginnings in a new type of men's magazine, led by *Loaded*. *Loaded* and its imitators were successful in swiftly ushering into the nation's psyche a new, ironic brand of male irresponsibility, championing as they did the delights of boozing, football and pornography. And by challenging the prescriptive manacles of political correctness, *Loaded* effectively kick-started the redefinition of young male culture in Britain. Before long, a new term for all this was coined: 'lad culture.'

In those early months, with its tongue firmly in its cheek, 'laddism' was a healthy and much-needed attack on the 'right-on' generation of graduates who were dominating the UK media. But soon lad culture itself began to get out of hand. As it seeped into television programming and commercials, and

Oliver Reed. **Revolver**

wove its way through offices, colleges and sports clubs, its irony was somehow lost, and it soon began to be tainted by the antiquated misogyny and homophobia that political correctness had sought to combat in the first place.

In the atmosphere of this misdirected machismo, Oliver Reed, who had made perhaps one decent film in twenty years, began to emerge again as an anti-hero for a new generation of men. Despite ongoing press disapproval and middle-England harrumphing over his lager-driven off-set antics, shameless misogyny and chaotic brawling, Reed was now someone to be viewed with a smirking affection, someone to be forgiven almost anything, someone to emulate on a 'weekend bender with the boys'. And although none of this helped his film career, there is no doubt that Oliver Reed was as famous in Britain in the last years of his life as he had been in his acting heyday. The tragic thing about all of it was that this fame rested on a handful of drunken TV appearances, and not on any worthwhile film roles.

On the ITV chat show *Aspel and Company* in 1986, Reed had staggered on, drunk and dishevelled, clutching a jug of what could have been vodka and orange. After a brief conversation that made no sense at all, he took to the stage and proceeded to growl the chorus of I'm A Wild One — complete with spastic gyrations — as the bemused backing band tried to keep up with him.

Several weeks later, in the US, Reed was in turn menacing, incomprehensible and downright surreal on *Late Night with David Letterman*. Asked about his drinking, the actor veered maniacally into a gibberish soliloquy about his diet: "I'm taking a high quantity, high porcelain diet. I drink a lot of cups, coffee cups. And I eat a lot of plates." By the time the show broke for a commercial break, Reed was shouting like a man possessed and Letterman looked scared for his life.

Notoriously, on the late night show, *After Dark*, in 1991, in what was clearly a recipe for disaster, Reed was invited to discuss 'Do men have to be violent?' with a group that included an American feminist, a military historian, a noted anthropologist and the daughter of a high profile mob boss. Broadcast live around midnight, *After Dark*'s premise was to assemble a disparate group of social commentators, sit them in armchairs in a comfy, darkened studio — access to a bar included — and have them talk freely about their chosen subject until the early hours of the morning.

Reed kicked off the proceedings by announcing that "a woman's role in society depends on whether she wants to get shafted", and things got worse from there. As the actor's language, general offensiveness and intimidation of the other guests intensified, the show's broadcaster, Channel 4, decided to pull it from the air mid-way through, and presented in its place an un-scheduled showing of a 1950s documentary on coal mining. The programme did come back on air twenty or so minutes later, however, just in time to see the now paralytic Reed planting a sloppy kiss on the cheek of the deeply unimpressed feminist. Reed ended the intellectual discussion by shouting at the show's extremely anxious crew: "Look, I'll put my plonker on the table if you don't give me a plate of mushy peas!"

Unsurprisingly, these increasingly absurd episodes were to strike a chord with the new generation of lads. Lad culture was essentially about wanting to conform, to be liked by mates, to be recognised and appreciated as a 'lager lout,' despite wearing a suit and holding down a responsible job, and despite having been brought up, more often than not, in safe suburban comfort by middle class parents. New lads would, in truth, have run a mile from true subversiveness. And deep down, Reed shared these exact sentiments. His behaviour was fuelled by an insecure desire to impress 'the boys', to be ac-cepted as a genuine hellraiser. But by his late forties the drinking and the brawling had got the better of him. Both Reed and his public seemed to have forgotten what he'd actually been good at in the first place.

An icon to pub culture he may have become, but Reed actually began life well-spoken and well-connected. Despite seeing his parents' marriage break down as a child, young Oliver was brought up cocooned by various female relatives and a succession of holiday nannies. Acting was in the child's blood. Reed's grandfather had been the actor-manager Sir Henry Beerbohm Tree, a high profile Victorian performer who had gone on to found the world-re-nowned Royal Academy of Dramatic Art (RADA). And little Oliver was also fortunate enough to call 'Uncle' one of Britain's greatest post-war filmmak-ers, Sir Carol Reed.

Although Oliver did go off the rails in his late teens, getting into fights in pubs and spending time in menial jobs, the call of the acting profession was inevitable. And although he spent a good few years hawking himself around the industry as an extra, success came pretty early. At twenty-three, Reed had secured his first major role — in Hammer's *Curse of the Werewolf* (1961).

Reed's apprenticeship with Hammer was just one of a number of shrewd and fortuitous partnerships that the actor forged. Hammer kept Reed largely on the sidelines, but the half a dozen B-movies they gave him helped him to hone his screen craft. After Hammer, Reed teamed with the up-and-coming Michael Winner and began to show versatility, star quality and fashionably flawed heroism in a sequence of films that probably represent the best work of Winner's career: *The System* (1964), *The Jokers* (1966*), I'll Never Forget*

What's'isname (1967) and *Hannibal Brooks* (1968). The actor then became an 'overnight' international star when his Uncle Carol, satisfied that his nephew had gained enough experience, cast him in the lavish *Oliver!* (1968), the last of the great Oscar-winning musicals of the sixties.

But it was with Ken Russell that Reed broke real ground as a leading man. On television, he brought a Byronic sensuality and an impetuous magnetism to his role of the composer in Russell's *The Debussy Film* (BBC 1966). In *Women in Love* (1969), he famously wrestled naked with Alan Bates in a scene that was unprecedented in mainstream cinema in its full-frontal frankness and audacious homo-eroticism, and which helped to further break down the walls of film censorship in Britain. And in the remarkable, hysterical and demonically decadent *The Devils* (1971), Reed held together a riotous feast of shrieking pyrotechnics with a performance of such control, emotion, pain and sensitivity that the scenes of his torture are still difficult to watch thirty years on.

As much as he liked to be one of the boys, Reed's errant socialising did not affect the trajectory of his first decade as a film star, and it is during this time that he proved himself to be Britain's most exhilarating box office draw. At his peak, regardless of nepotism or good connections, Reed had a screen presence that surpassed that of his British contemporaries and placed him in a class of his own. Exuding quiet danger, or a winning charm, he could portray malevolent villainy, heroic integrity, lower class boorishness, high class refinement, worthy disillusionment, cockiness, charisma and churlishness with equal aplomb.

As the seventies started, Reed was Britain's most highly paid actor. He held onto this pole position with hard, uncompromising films such as Douglas Hickox's *Sitting Target* (1972) and popular fodder with a fashionable edge: *The Three Musketeers* (1973), *The Four Musketeers* (1974), *Tommy* (1975).

He could have been more famous still. In 1969, Reed was considered for James Bond after Sean Connery had departed, somewhat acrimoniously, from the franchise. It may be difficult to equate the later rambling, grizzled chat show figure with Fleming's suave killing machine, but there is no doubt that at the time Reed could have both looked and played the part. And he could have deepened Connery's dark appeal, matched his virility, and infused Bond with more of the ruthless danger of the original novels. But it never transpired. Reed, it was reported, lost out on Bond for the reason that he was too famous already; his screen persona was too well known.

The real reason for Reed losing out on Bond, it has been speculated, has more to do with the actor's increasingly public bad behaviour, not least his highly visible extra-marital affair with a ballet dancer, Jacqui Daryl (for whom he eventually left his first wife.). It seems that, as soon as his career really began, Reed's damaging reputation for off-screen mischief had already taken a foothold in the nation's consciousness. Nevertheless, it is likely that Reed would have soon grown tired of the role of Bond (although perhaps not as quickly as Lazenby did), and would have felt constrained by any long-term commitment to the character.

Oliver Reed and Susan George. **Venom**

By 1975, Reed's level of fame could not be sustained by living and working in Britain. The declining film industry and Draconian income tax levy were making it impossible for a star of his magnitude to remain in the country and prosper. Unsurprisingly, this was a time of A-list movie star exodus. Michael Caine, Peter Sellers, Sean Connery — all left UK shores for Spain or Switzerland or LA, and were now working more frequently in Hollywood or on the Continent. Reed, however, fearful of losing his drinking mates and afternoon sessions in the pub, and distrustful of the Hollywood hierarchy, refused to budge.

It wasn't as if he hadn't had offers. According to his biographer, Reed turned down both *The Sting* (1973) and *Jaws* (1975) — with both roles going to Robert Shaw and consolidating Shaw's international stardom. (Shaw's biographer's version, not surprisingly, differs from this, claiming that Shaw was first choice for both parts.) But, as Reed and his close friends would have known themselves, Oliver would not have been able to play the Hollywood game. The etiquette pervading Hollywood stardom is far more conservative than the scandal sheets would have us believe. Reed would never have toed the studio line, or showed the correct level of deference to the right people.

But by opting to stay in Britain, Reed effectively threw away the level of movie stardom he had been enjoying. From 1976, the quality of the films he appeared in plunged dramatically, and his roles within them quickly fell from leading man to character support: *Burnt Offerings* (1976), *The Prince and the Pauper* (1977), *The Class of Miss McMichael* (1978), *Venom* (1981), *Condorman* (1981). That he remained busy is inarguable, but not one of these films was worth five minutes of *The Devils* or *Women in Love*. In the space of a few years, Reed turned from Britain's biggest film star to little more than a jobbing actor.

It was also during this time that Reed's reputation as an untamed, insatiable hellraiser began to run riot. He wasn't the first, and he won't be the last, but Reed raised hell so consistently, so predictably and so destructively that people started to recoil from him. All this may have become cheerful anecdotal fodder if Reed had been an amusing drunk — but, in essence, he wasn't. There is something of a raucous charm to the debauched exploits of George Best or Peter Cook or Keith Moon; there is something gently affecting about the tipsy misadventures of Dean Martin or David Niven. But Reed's drunkenness unleashed a cold-eyed, vicious, paranoid animal. Shy, quiet and unassuming when sober, Reed when drunk became a volatile, unpredictable, intimidating monster. Even his friend Michael Winner commented: "There was no greater pendulum swing in any human being that I've ever met than Oliver Reed sober to Oliver Reed drunk."

Of course, there is a wealth of funny stories arising from Reed's inebriation. There is the time he arrived at Galway airport lying on the baggage conveyor; the time he punched out the lights in his kitchen because he couldn't find the switch; the time he shed his clothes at a swanky Madrid hotel, climbed into the giant aquarium and started swallowing goldfish whole; the time he dived out of a first-floor hotel window into the swimming pool; the time he welcomed his daughter's German boyfriend into his house, having especially festooned it with Union Jacks …

But for every amusing anecdote there appears to be hostile malevolence lurking just behind the hi-jinks, always waiting to attack as the merriment turned to complete intoxication. And all too often, this behaviour was laced with a vitriolic snobbishness that was markedly at odds with Reed's 'one of the boys' image.

Entertaining journalist Jane Parsons and her fiancé over Sunday lunch in a busy pub, Reed turned from exquisite charmer to enraged monster over the course of a few drinks, starting with offensive potshots at Parsons' 'crap' engagement ring and steel-eyed taunts of "you're just common fucking rubbish … you're a nobody", leaving his guests embarrassed, humiliated and not a little scared. Reed's sister-in-law later confirmed that Oliver "didn't like women to contradict him. If they did he would get very abusive and very nasty. In that situation he was a very frightening man."

ARRIBA . AL FINAL DE LA ESCALERA DE ESTA TETRICA MANSION . HAY UNA PUERTA ENCADENADA . DONDE VIVE . ALGO HORRIBLE . DIABOLICO Y ESPANTOSO!

KAREN BLACK
OLIVER REED
BETTE DAVIS

PESADILLA DIABOLICA

DIRECTOR: DANS CURTIS   TECHNICOLOR

Such schizophrenic turnabouts in Reed's behaviour may have been more tolerable if they hadn't been reinforced by the actor's powerful physical presence. For when the danger, the menace and the sneering paranoia took hold after a few bottles, Reed could become, by all accounts, a terrifying force.

After his friend Stephen Ford had told him a few home truths one time, Reed hurled him into a bed of thorns. Ford was wearing only swimming trunks. Reed then continued to chase him almost off a cliff. After they made up, Ford had his cuts attended to in the bathroom by Reed's then partner, only to set the actor off again with accusations of "What are you doing with my woman? Fuck you, Ford! Come on out!"

More damagingly, a drinking bout with his long-time minder, Reg Prince, got out of hand when, according to Prince, Reed threw him off a restaurant balcony, severely damaging his spine. Prince, however, was not exactly the shy, retiring type himself, and the subsequent litigation failed to prove what had actually happened that night. Nevertheless, the incident saw a close, decade-long friendship come to an end.

Four Musketeers   *1B*

Oliver Reed is Athos in 20th Century-Fox's all star production of "The Four Musketeers," premiering .... at the .... Theatre.

What is most dismaying about Reed's 'dark side' is that it was so totally at odds with the professional and conscientiously polite persona he projected when sober. As with Dr Jekyll and his evil potion, the demon drink had the same effect on Reed. The journalist Denis Meikle described this revealingly after a 1992 trip to Reed's then home, in Guernsey, to interview the actor about his Hammer days.

During the afternoon, Reed was courtesy itself, generously furnishing the visiting interviewer with comprehensive and expansive recollections of his early days as a film actor. Meikle commented that the actor was "complimentary, eager to please, and respondent to questions with patience and in that soft mellifluous tone of voice that was as famous as his face."

So impressed was the interviewer that he offered to meet up with Reed and his wife later to buy them a drink. As soon as they reconvened, however, Meikle sensed he was in the presence of a different man. With them "came a disturbing air," the writer commented, "as though all of us had inadvertently woken to find ourselves in the middle of a film by David Lynch." Reed had been drinking all afternoon, and Meikle noted, was now in the process

Oliver Reed stars as Jean La Bete in *THE TRAP*, an exciting and dramatic film set in the wilds of British Columbia during the mid-nineteenth century. La Bete is a giant of a man, strong in character and physical brute force, yet tender when the occasion demands. Starring opposite him is Rita Tushingham as Eve, an orphaned mute bondsmaiden. *THE TRAP* is a George Brown production for world-wide distribution by the Rank Organisation. Sidney Hayers directed.
TRA-1 (S/C)

of transforming from courteous Oliver into hellraising 'Ollie'.

The interviewer put up his guard and prepared to spend the rest of the evening on tenterhooks. He noticed that Reed's young second wife, Josephine, sat passively at her husband's side. "In his present mood, Oliver required to be appeased, pandered to, and obeyed. The consequences of failing to do so risked a wrath that was more than capable of sweeping all that was before it ..." he wrote.

Reed's mood continued to swing from buoyant to aggressive, and the interviewer and his wife found themselves going back, with an entourage of hangers-on, to Reed's own custom-built 'English pub'. It was here that Meikle noticed that "the metamorphosis from man to animal was now complete." Reed kicked off the proceedings by stabbing a hunting knife into the bar, inches away from the interviewer's forearm, and then staring him out like a possessed predator stalking his prey. The evening descended from there. Some time later, when Reed noticed Meikle's pregnant wife inadvertently yawn, he was outraged, and had the couple forcefully ejected from the house.

Meikle summed up his meeting with the star thus: "The man I met in 1992 was no jovial, fun-loving, one-of-the-boys, as his contemporaries would like to have it. He was an alcoholic, pure and simple.... [He] was not a figure of fun.... He was a tragic figure, who destroyed himself utterly."

Indeed, in the last years of his life, Reed seemed to have alienated the rest of the film industry with his behaviour. His *Oliver!* co-star Mark Lester noticed that, after a recording of the TV show *This is Your Life*, on which

Lester and Reed were among the guests celebrating Ron Moody's career, Reed stood alone in the bar, clearly aware but not at all fazed that nobody wanted anything to do with him. Lee Evans noticed the same thing when working with Reed on *Funny Bones* (1995). More damagingly, producers and directors were becoming less prepared to take a risk on Reed's destructive off-set behaviour.

The actor's reputation wasn't helped when he was fired from the multi-million dollar Renny Harlin/Geena Davis romp, *Cutthroat Island* (1995), before filming had even begun. Reportedly, during an introductory dinner with the film's executives and cast members, Reed managed to offend a number of key people — Geena Davis included — by dropping his pants to show off the eagle's talons he had tattooed on his penis. The next day, unable to remember what he had actually done, Reed was flown home from the set as quickly as he had arrived, knowing only that he had been fired for 'inappropriate behaviour relating to alcohol'.

Reed's career stumbled on with some obscure German movies and one more collaboration with Michael Winner — the execrable *Parting Shots* (1998) — and it looked set to collapse in on itself when he was offered a redemptive, and rather lucrative, role in Ridley Scott's *Gladiator*. However, Scott did not cast Reed without interviewing the star three times and making him read — such was the risk of employing an unpredictable personality.

But Reed did get the role and, in March 1999, set off for Valletta, Malta, to shoot his scenes for the $120 million movie. True to form, he immediately sought out the most inviting bars, and rarely spent less than £150 a time in them.

The Malta shoot went without too much incident, until May 2, when Reed and his wife Josephine stopped off at an English-style pub for a lunchtime tipple. Starting on strong German beer, Reed was excited by the arrival of a party of sailors, whereupon he stood up and announced: "Black rum all round!" By 2.30pm, according to Reed's biographer, Oliver had downed twelve double measures of Jamaican rum on top of the eight bottles of German beer he had had before the sailors arrived. Shortly after ordering a whisky, the actor fell forward and began breathing erratically. An ambulance arrived and rushed him to St Luke's Hospital, where, after fifteen minutes of trying to revive his arrested heart, Oliver Reed was pronounced dead. He was sixty-one.

Nobody was particularly surprised that Reed died this way. In fact, that he had reached sixty-one seemed something of an achievement. But what did emerge in the newspaper reports and obituaries in the weeks that followed his death was a sense of sadness over a career sacrificed to hellraising, a lament for the wasted years. Ridley Scott paid the actor a great tribute by redeeming his *Gladiator* character's role (formerly a 'baddie') and shooting extras scenes utilising a body double, out-take footage and computer-generated imagery, at a reported extra cost of $2 million. Had Reed lived, however, his character might not have needed redeeming to kick-start his career again, as *Gladiator* became, of course, a huge hit. But Reed's touched-up performance became his most significant screen appearance since *Castaway* in 1986 — it even landed him a posthumous Oscar nomination.

Whether Reed, had he lived, would have successfully harnessed this career revival or not is arguable. He may have slipped back into all-night drinking sessions at his local pub and continued to finance them with the kind of garbage he had been walking through for the last twenty years. He may have seized the moment and begun to make the big important films he had eschewed in the mid seventies. But whatever direction his life might otherwise have taken, with a drink at hand, Ollie Reed's Mr Hyde would never have been too far away.

[Oliver Reed filmography p.139]

Diana Dors
The Lakes Regress

When she met Alan Lake in 1968, Diana Dors was no stranger to turbulence in her life, or to humiliation in her career. Already, at thirty-seven, she'd suffered failure in Hollywood, tabloid scandal, two abortions, two failed marriages, separation from her children, weight problems and bankruptcy. But where this might have finished off plenty of more fragile celebrities — driving them to despair, drink and maybe even suicide — Diana Dors was still very much around, the archetypal survivor.

From her beginnings as a cocky, sharp-tongued, drama-schooled 'British Monroe' to her subsequent omnipresent tabloid status as a thick-skinned, fat-cushioned, bullishly maternal self-promoter, Diana Dors always had the knack of playing the British public like a harpsichord. Since her first brush with real fame, she had rarely been out of the public eye. And when not appearing in films or splashed over the front pages of the newspapers, she was guesting indiscriminately on television panel games and chat shows.

But by 1968 Diana Dors' career as a film star was effectively over. To the serious side of the entertainment industry, she had become something of a peroxide joke. But she still had a few tricks up her sleeve.

Headstrong and driven, she had been in films since 1947, and made a minor but not insignificant impression in David Lean's masterful *Oliver Twist* (1948). The Rank Film Organisation, Britain's staid, ration-book answer to a Hollywood studio, responded by putting her under contract, and she dutifully played starlet parts in a number of forgettable movies until its 'Charm School' (essentially a production line for plum-in-the-mouth platinum beauties) closed in 1950. Hungry for real stardom, Diana then married Dennis Hamilton, an entrepreneurial rough diamond type with a talent for press manipulation. This seemed to work. Hamilton had a bit of a temper, to put it lightly, and his behaviour ensured she remained in the headlines even when her films bombed at the box office. (At their wedding ceremony, Hamilton threatened to beat up the registrar.) Diana continued making drossy pictures and falling further into debt, but Hamilton kept her profile high with bad boy antics and by surrounding her with ostentatious riches that the couple couldn't really afford.

But Diana was actually a very competent actress and a lot more intelligent than some of her eye candy contemporaries. She finally got the chance to shine in J Lee Thompson's anti capital punishment drama, *Yield to the Night* (1956). Although no raging international success, the film propelled her to Hollywood, where RKO offered to put her under contract, just as Rank had done.

Within days of arriving in LA, Hamilton ensured the US showbiz press was aware of his wife's presence when he beat up a photographer at Diana's own introductory party. (The snapper, it has to be said, had pushed them into the pool for a photo opportunity.) Hollywood may have been Babylon below the surface, but surface was all-important, and the couple found themselves kept at arm's length after that incident. Consequently, the films that RKO put Diana in were as unremarkable as the potboilers she'd made ten years earlier.

Disillusioned with Hollywood, Diana returned to Britain in the late fifties and launched herself unsurely as a cabaret act. This eventually flourished, albeit for a short time. Her marriage to Hamilton had, in the meantime, broken down, amid much headline grabbing (he died of syphilis, of all things, in 1959) and she hooked up with a struggling comedian called Richard Dawson. Her film career, however, was going nowhere fast. In 1960, she announced that she wasn't going to make any more 'stinkers'. She then promptly appeared in *Scent of Mystery*, a third-rate novelty hokum filmed in 'Smell-O-Vision' and exhibited using a process that wafted different aromas around the theatre.

More forgettable films followed. By the time she met Alan Lake, Diana had married and divorced Dawson (who went on to have tremendous success on US television) and had been reduced to hawking her variety act, which she'd first performed in Las Vegas, around the somewhat less glamorous clubs in the English provinces.

Alan Lake, by contrast, had a clean slate in 1968, and was unblemished by the razor-edged glitter that ostentatious fame had showered on Diana. Indeed, he appeared to be going places. He was, self-consciously, a product of the intense, virile school of acting. From a working class background (in Stoke-on-Trent), he had started by emulating the path of the recent generation of acting greats — Richard Burton, Richard Harris, Peter O' Toole, Albert Finney — from the humdrum drone of blue collar towns to the sound of RADA applause. Although he had as yet secured no high profile roles, what little he had done on television and on the big screen marked him as a new talent to watch. Lake had a potentially bright future as a 'serious actor'. And offscreen, he matched this raw energy with a capacity for drinking that, even before his fame, was fast becoming legendary.

Diana Dors met Lake on the set of a formula British cop show in 1968 (*The Inquisitor*, which ultimately wasn't transmitted as the show was later scrapped) and within six weeks she was married to him. Within a year, she'd given birth to their son, Jason. The betrothal sparked a positive reaction which, albeit temporarily, fuelled both their careers. Diana was at that time bankrupt, despite living opulently in a Berkshire farmhouse. By joining up with the young actor — new wave, dangerous, brooding, intense — she had managed to reinvent herself yet again. And Lake couldn't have been further from the ersatz glamour of Rank and Dennis Hamilton, or from the oily vaudeville of Las Vegas and Dickie Dawson.

Indeed, the couple seemed scheduled for better things as the seventies began. In January 1970, they began starring together, to great acclaim, in a play by Donald Howarth called *Three Months Gone*. Lake played a boarding house lodger; Diana his vampish landlady. For the first time since *Yield to the Night*, Diana's reviews for an acting role were almost unanimously ecstatic. The play was transferred from the Royal Court in Sloane Square to the West End. As the new decade got under way, it seemed that Diana was transforming her life from an emotional and professional disaster area to that of one half of a successful acting union. If they were never going to scale the heights of Vivien Leigh and Laurence Olivier, Dors and Lake might at least have become, albeit very briefly, something of a downmarket Burton and Taylor. Other offers for the couple to work together started to pour in, including more theatre work and a sitcom for Yorkshire television, *Queenie's Castle*.

But the acclaim and domestic bliss was not to last. Lake may have been blessed with some natural talent and gypsy good looks, but he couldn't match it with sense or good fortune. And his fondness for boozing and brawling immediately hampered his career. In July 1970, still playing in *Three Months Gone*, Lake and his friend, pop star 'Leapy' Lee Graham (his Little Arrows reached No. 2 in the UK in 1968), were involved in 'an altercation' at their local pub. Glasses were smashed, punches were thrown, and Leapy knifed the landlord. The police were called in, and Lake and Leapy were charged with GBH and causing malicious damage.

Although these were serious charges, Lake had not used the knife himself. Nevertheless, a witness claimed to have seen him hand the knife to Leapy. Perhaps the first true instance of the bad luck that was to dog Lake's career for the rest of his life came when the judge sentenced him to eighteen months in prison instead of the suspended sentence he was expecting. Leapy Lee got three years. Dors and Lake were stunned. Instead of joining Diana for the recording of *Queenie's Castle* in Leeds, Lake found himself behind bars, and not the ones he was used to leaning on.

Diana went about her work commitments and Lake ended up serving twelve months. Yet, despite this appalling setback, the couple were in a positive frame of mind when he was released in October 1971. If anything, the stint inside may have added to Lake's macho appeal, and Diana was doing well with *Queenie's Castle*, which was shaping up to be one of the better ITV

Early portrait of Diana Dors

sitcoms of the period. With Diana's knack for survival, it looked like they had weathered this storm. As a welcome home present, she bought Lake a "beautiful, seventeen-hand mare called Sapphire". Six months later, out riding the horse, Lake broke his back when it ran into the bough of a tree.

The doctors told Lake to prepare for life in a wheelchair. Remarkably, he recovered, and within weeks was walking again, although in extreme pain. But the psychological effects were more profound. With another long period of unemployment looming, he hit the bottle with a vengeance.

Ironically, Diana's career was providing some real highlights during this time, albeit in lower profile roles. Aside from *Queenie's Castle*, she had refocused herself in character parts, and was turning in some good work. As a towel-clad, bloated nymphomaniac, molesting John Moulder-Brown in a sauna room, she contributes a great scene to Jerzy Skolimowski's darkly comic, swimming pool-set *Deep End* (1970), even though she's only on screen for a couple of minutes. Similarly, she livens up *Hannie Caulder* (1971), *The Amazing Mr. Blunden* (1972) and holds her own with a stellar British cast, orgiastically receiving a brutal massage from Vincent Price in the infectiously lively *Theatre of Blood* (1973). And in 1974, she amazed highbrow theatre critics by accepting the role of Jocasta in Keith Michell's production of *Oedipus* at the Chichester Festival. But this was typical Diana Dors — if she was ever a fallen star, she never stayed in the gutter for long.

Alan Lake, however, could not pick himself up so easily. As he drank more and more to fill the time and heal the pain, Lake came to resent his wife's ongoing success. In one of her memoirs, *Dors by Diana*, the actress recalls

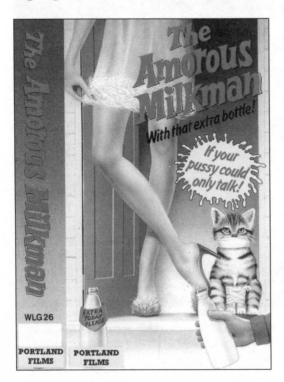

how "having exhausted myself in the role of Jocasta, I returned home to find myself having to cope with the tyrant Oedipus again, only now in private. I was even forced to call a doctor to help me deal with him, for alcohol had unleashed a monster, uncontrollable and frightening."

Lake's increasingly frequent drunken rages were not entirely governed by jealousy. He also seemed to be lapsing periodically into psychotic episodes. Dors recalled that, on a family holiday in France, Lake's drinking also began "producing hallucinations about who he'd been in a previous life". After another bout, he started "screaming that he was a soldier called Jimmy, lying in the muddy trenches of France during the First World War".

Lake was clearly heading for disaster. He tried to save himself by launching head-first into Roman Catholicism. Diana followed him into the Church, and some months of calm followed. In November 1974, Diana was struck down by a life-threatening bout of meningitis. Having rushed her to hospital, Lake was told she might not last the night. He fainted. But Diana pulled through, and early in 1975, fell pregnant again at the age of forty-three.

Medical sense dictated that Diana should have a termination, given her age and her recent brush with

Diana Dors

death, but the couple's newfound allegiance to Catholicism prevented this. And two abortions that Diana had previously had had left a wound of guilt that she didn't want re-opening. But in light of what the couple had been through in the previous years, it seems insane that they should set themselves up for the heartbreak of losing a baby. Nevertheless, they did set themselves up, and they did lose the baby, in August 1975. Diana weathered this with her characteristic pragmatism; Lake went back to the bottle.

In the years that followed, both Dors' and Lake's acting careers went into freefall. To keep busy, both were reduced to co-starring in the cheap and smutty soft-core comedies that were so inexplicably popular in Britain during the seventies. Somehow, it wasn't really a shock to see Diana bluster her way through *The Amorous Milkman* (1974), *Swedish Wildcats* (1974), *Bedtime for Rosie* (1974) and *Keep It Up Downstairs* (1976) — her career had for years hinged on livening up dross or sending herself up, despite the accolades of the early seventies. But to see Lake mugging so humourlessly in some of the same films seemed somehow more tragic. Only three or four years after his professional career had kicked off, he was consigned to some of the most abysmal films Britain has ever produced. By *Confessions from the David Galaxy Affair* (1979), he was approaching the end of his tether. Overacting wildly, Lake tries to liven up the flat (i.e. sexless) scenes with some dubious end-of-the-pier variety shtick, which is largely good-natured, but, more often than not, painfully embarrassing to watch. To add to his humiliation, he is deftly acted off the screen by Glynn Edwards, whose clipped-talking, seen-it-all sleuth provides, in its quiet way, the only real humour in the film.

In 1980, Diana left the almost continually drunk Lake for a period, claiming that life had become "public humiliation for both of us wherever we went, in the end, I refused to be seen with him." They were reconciled when Lake promised to undergo treatment for his alcoholism.

While Lake thrashed around in the grip of the grog, Diana continued to pay the bills by writing no less than three best-selling memoirs, appearing in a good tea-time TV adaptation of Richmal Crompton's *Just William* books, and launching a new career as a chat show host. Acting now apparently taking very much a back seat, she prepared to face the eighties as a media jack-of-all-trades, a role that was quickly consolidated by appearing in the video for the Adam Ant single Prince Charming, becoming an agony aunt for the *Daily Star* and, in 1983, joining the burgeoning breakfast TV channel, TV-AM, to present a slot about dieting. Lake, however, had hardly any work at all. For him, as Dors' biographer Damon Wise comments, "1983 was already an empty book."

But by now, Diana's health was seriously failing, even if she did continue to bounce back and carry on working. In June 1982 she'd been rushed to hospital after collapsing with stomach pains. An ovarian cyst had burst and the operation revealed that cancerous tissue was surrounding it. This was removed, and she returned to the treadmill. In September 1983, she had another operation for the removal of more cancerous tissue. Again, she returned to work, even to acting, with a role in what was to be director Joseph Losey's last film, *Steaming* (1984), a static drama of feminine camaraderie set in a Turkish bath house. When the film wrapped in April 1984, she collapsed once again.

This time, an operation revealed that the cancer had spread throughout her body, and was at an inoperable level. On May 4, 1984, at the age of fifty-three, Diana Dors died. A devastated Lake prepared a statement for waiting journalists. "I lost my wife and a soulmate," he wrote. Her obituary in *The Times* (May 7, 1984) said, fittingly: "Stardom may have long since disappeared, but she was still, undeniably, a celebrity."

Lake fell, characteristically, into an immediate and unforgiving depression. He did nothing to alleviate this by wandering about the empty house he'd shared with Diana, without work and having alienated everyone but his closest companions. On October 10, 1984, having taken son Jason to the train station, Lake took a shotgun into Jason's empty bedroom and put it to his left temple. It was the sixteenth anniversary of the day he and Diana had met. The housekeeper heard the shot and ran up to find the forty-three-year-old actor dead on the bedroom floor. Minutes before, he'd sat in despair after speaking to prospective viewers of the house on the phone. He'd said to the housekeeper "I am in more trouble than you will ever know."

Alan Lake's career never got to the point where it could be taken seriously, and for that he had both himself and his desperately bad luck to blame. His face is now synonymous with the seedy films he made in the late seventies and his image is one of sideburns, shirt open to the navel, chest hair, medallion and a cheesy, lecherous grin. Things may have turned out differently for him if he had harnessed his obvious passion and channelled it into something artistically positive. He certainly had the torment, the looks and the aggression to elicit an intense presence. But he was a desperate actor in a desperate decade. And jobbing British film actors took anything that was available in the seventies.

Diana Dors, by contrast, is still regarded as something of a kitschy legend, still held close in the affections of her ageing public. In her later years, she emitted a brash cuddliness with a hint of sexual allure, something akin to catnip to the robustly unerotic British public. She was like a fat, glamorous dinner lady you could share a joke with as you queued up for your grub at school. In 2000, a British TV film dramatised her life, particularly the turbulent years with Lake, and met with general audience approval. It was trashy, soapy, glitzy stuff — exactly how Diana would have liked it.

[*Diana Dors filmography p.142*]

Mary Millington
True Blues

It could be said that the two 'hottest' British sex film stars of the seventies were, at best, only average looking and completely free of acting talent. In fact, to say that Fiona Richmond was average looking is something of a compliment, but she did at least know how to play the sex industry game to her advantage, and what she lacked in looks and dramatic ability she more than made up for in confidence and savvy. And when the steamy roles dried up, Richmond was shrewd enough to make sure she was gainfully employed in other fields, or at least well provided for.

The other, Mary Millington, was not quite so self-assured. But, in her case, it was a simple vulnerability and a good natured promiscuity that appealed the hordes of male fans that bought her magazines and flocked to her flaccid sex films. Tragically, though, these were also the very qualities that led to her downfall.

Having drifted into glamour modelling in the late sixties, Mary Maxted, a young housewife from Dorking, soon fell in with the infamous pornographer John Lindsay and began racking up appearances in hardcore porn loops, 8mm reels of which sold well all over Europe. One of the first loops Mary made was called *Miss Borehole* (1970), the title giving a fairly accurate

*Mary advertising back copies of **Whitehouse** (on
what looks like the Fawlty Towers set!).*

impression of the activities the film depicts. No actress, but certainly not a
shy performer, Mary featured twenty or so of these loops before returning to
glamour modelling for established magazines such as *Knave* and *Men Only*.
At this point, her career was indistinguishable from the hundreds of other
models who dabbled in explicit stag movies and men's magazines. But then
she met David Sullivan.

David Sullivan is known in Britain today for being the proprietor of the
outrageously sex-soaked tabloid comedy newspapers, the *Sunday Sport* and
the *Daily Sport*. But long before the sordid hysterics of the *Sport* graced
the news stands, Sullivan had already established himself, at twenty-six,
as Britain's premier porn publisher, a kind of precocious hybrid of William
Randolph Hearst and Larry Flynt. When Mary met him in 1975 they became
lovers (despite her continuing marriage), and under Sullivan's tutelage, Mary

soon came to personify the cheerfully sordid underbelly of Britain in the seventies.

Sullivan's magazines, *Whitehouse* and *Private* were the most explicit on the British market at the time, and they benefited from a raunchy provincialism that spoke directly to working class males in industrial towns. (The publisher also had an appealingly mischievous subversive streak. His strongest title, *Whitehouse*, was named after Mary Whitehouse, the pious, die-hard campaigner for family values who was the bane of 'permissiveness', and the liberal media's presentation of it, for forty years.) Perhaps most importantly, the girls in Sullivan's magazines did not seem unattainable. They were not panther-like beauties, bathed in soft focus lovedust. Quite the opposite — the models in *Whitehouse* were the kind of greasy-haired pixies you might meet outside the chip shop on a Saturday night.

Always a tactical player, Sullivan shrewdly introduced Mary to his readership by claiming she was the nymphomaniacal, bisexual sister of *Whitehouse*'s nominal editor, Doreen Millington. Thus he changed Mary's name and set her on the path to notoriety.

Sullivan was nothing if not ambitious, and with his publishing empire thriving (he had launched two more magazines before the end of 1975), he decided to branch out into film production. Mary had taken off as his number one model, the 'Doreen's naughty sister' business clearly striking a chord with the magazine's more gullible readers. Now Sullivan took it upon himself to make her an adult film star.

Today's adult film stars are not likely to be widely known by the general public, occupying as they do a place in a relatively specialist (albeit lucrative) video-based market. But in the seventies, things were different. When, in the US, *Deep Throat* broke new ground in 1972 by playing in major theatres in major cities, the resulting *cause célèbre* made a household name of Linda Lovelace. Two years later, almost everyone with a smattering of interest in the cinema knew of a Dutch actress called Sylvia Kristel, thanks to the international success of *Emmanuelle*. And in the second half of the seventies, the domestic soft porn film was pretty much the only kind of film generating any

money in Britain, despite the fact that it was heavily regulated and, more often than not, copiously censored. So it seemed feasible that Sullivan *could* make a 'film star' out of Mary Millington by featuring her in the kind of weary skin-fests that were packing out the Odeons. And, with some expert marketing, he did.

Mary had secured some walk-on parts in tame British skinflicks at the close of her hardcore days, but this was going precisely nowhere before Sullivan took control of her career. She had made no impression whatsoever in these 'legitimate' movies, and had quite rightly come to the conclusion that acting was not her forte. But when he put up the money for *Come Play With Me* (1977), Sullivan was single-handedly taking the reins of the British sex film industry, and he propelled Mary to the forefront of it without demanding anything resembling acting from her.

A creaky music hall travesty starring Alfie Bass and Irene Handl — wrinkled comedy performers with lengthy pedigrees in variety vehicles — *Come Play With Me* justified itself as a sex film by weaving static scenes of nude aerobics and sauna shenanigans through a narrative that concerns two fugitive ignoramuses (Bass and director Harrison Marks) hiding from the law at a health farm, wherein a bevy of nubile nurses attend to their every 'need'. Given the numbing crassness of the whole project, the domestic success that it went on to achieve is nothing less than staggering. *Come Play With Me* ran continuously for four years at one London cinema. And when it closed in London, it became one of the UK's first sizeable video hits. This was due in no small way to Sullivan's marketing of the film as a vehicle for Mary Millington, trailing it extensively (and quite fraudulently, hinting that it was 'hardcore') in his magazines. The ploy worked better than he could have expected.

Yet Mary is barely in the film, and when she is, she is indistinguishable from the other models on show. In little more than a walk-on, she turns up, strips off and struggles with a minimal amount of dialogue. But this didn't seem to bother the punters. *Come Play With Me* ended up grossing a reported £5 million on an investment of £120,000.

Not surprisingly, Sullivan immediately rushed another film into production, with a larger role for Mary. *The Playbirds* (1978) sees her as a policewoman going undercover as a nude model to catch a serial killer, a hackneyed plot borrowed from a score of lurid potboilers, not least the Harry H. Corbett thriller, *Cover Girl Killer* (1959). As a snapshot of the dying days of the British soft porn industry, however, *The Playbirds* is not uninteresting. Sadly, Mary is terrible in it. Somewhat unfairly, she is required to handle dialogue scenes with professional actors such as Glynn Edwards, Windsor Davies and Gavin Campbell (later to become a well-known face on BBC TV's *That's Life*), the effect of which is embarrassing to the extreme. Struggling to make even a single word sound convincing, to say that she is stilted and ill-at-ease would be paying her a compliment. But it still didn't matter. With Sullivan's road-tested marketing strategy, *The Playbirds* cleaned up as well.

It is quite bizarre, but also revealing, that as well as taking more significant parts in Sullivan's films and featuring prominently in his magazines, Mary

Millington often stood behind the counters of her mentor's sex shops, principally the Whitehouse Shop in Norbury, meeting punters face to face and attending to everyday transactions. More disturbingly, she appeared to fall into prostitution just as readily. There are reports of Mary working, from her earliest modelling days, as a high class call girl. Curiously, none of this more demeaning work stopped when she achieved a degree of the fame and fortune she had always craved.

It is perhaps not surprising then, given her willingness to be exploited and objectified for any apparent commercial end, to discover that Mary had some deep-seated issues that had irreversibly damaged her self-esteem. She was born illegitimately and grew up fatherless and ostracised at school. She married very young and nursed her terminally ill mother for more than a decade, paying for her care by drifting into porn. She was prone to neurosis

Alfresco flashing. Mary Millington at the height of her modelling days.

and morbidity, traits that were eventually exacerbated by increasing drug use — cocaine being, then as now, the fashionable narcotic for the media set.

When her mother died in 1976, Mary had become more noticeably unstable. Preoccupied with death, she reportedly embarked on a training course to be a mortician, but could not endure the studying. She then investigated running a funeral home, but nothing came of that idea. Either way, this was not the sort of behaviour one would expect from the country's hottest porn pin-up.

Her love affair with Sullivan at an end due to her increasing unpredictability, the two nonetheless continued their professional partnership. But Mary turned thirty-three in November 1978, and was becoming all too aware that her modelling career would not last much longer. She began to find herself making way for new, younger talent in Sullivan's stable of magazines, and she was unable to rely on a burgeoning career as a performer. Indeed, in Sullivan's next film, the monumentally ill-conceived *Confessions from the David Galaxy Affair* (1979), she was required only for an extended cameo.

By now, the soft porn theatrical film was on its way out in Britain. *David Galaxy* was Sullivan's first flop; he subsequently began to focus on shorter

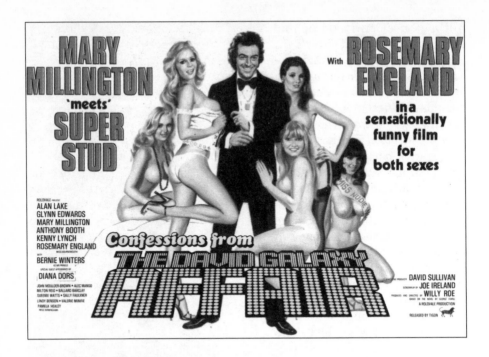

films for easy transfer to video anthologies. Knowing that she did not have the ability to make the crossover into mainstream acting, this refocusing of her mentor's attention pushed Mary further into instability.

Mary instead devoted more time to working in her own shop, but her growing paranoia also began to jeopardise this enterprise. Her premises were raided a number of times, perhaps not unusually for the era; Mary also claimed that she was being threatened and abused by the police, and forced to pay protection money. Whether this was true or not, the Metropolitan Police Force's vice squad is certainly known to have suffered from widespread corruption in the seventies. Later internal investigations revealed some highly suspect behaviour on the part of its detectives, all of which gives some credibility to Mary's claims. Nevertheless, her own reckless attitude to running a business did not help matters, as she brazenly sold the kind of outlawed material that was bound to land her in trouble sooner or later.

To justify flying in the face of the country's obscenity laws, Mary trotted out some well-rehearsed arguments about freedom of choice and sexual liberation, but, to be fair, her talent as a political spokesperson was probably on a par with her grasp of serious acting. And by this time, she was far from strong enough mentally to take on the establishment.

In early 1979, her ghost written 'autobiography' was issued. Despite being tailored squarely for the undemanding *Whitehouse* reader and spinning a web of overheated fantasy that would not have been out of place in a Jackie Collins novel, *The Amazing Mary Millington* does offer the occasional insight into her troubled psyche. The stigma of being born illegitimately and the low self-esteem that dominated her childhood and teenage years are frequently alluded to. Similarly, there is the morbid fixation with death and illness (in the form of repeated references to her mother's drawn out battle with cancer, and the warnings from self-appointed moral guardians that Mary's life will end in tragedy and suicide). Most of the book, however, goes in for porn mag wish fulfilment scenarios — lethargic descriptions of sexual encounters which, with their soft-focus glow and travelogue leanings, look like they come straight from the script of an *Emmanuelle* sequel.

When it isn't whipping its male readers up into a frenzy, *The Amazing Mary Millington* repetitively hammers home trite arguments for 'freedom of expression' and a review of the obscenity laws. (Somewhat desperately, the last forty pages of the book are devoted to "an extract from the National Campaign for the Reform of the Obscene Publications Act's report to the government on obscenity and censorship", an incongruously heavy and prohibitively dry dissection of the laws governing censorship in Britain and around the world. This is informative in its way, but laughably unnecessary as a postscript to what is essentially a porno potboiler.)

Nevertheless, the very deception of *The Amazing Mary Millington* is salient as an indication of the conflict between Mary's 'available' exterior and the interior truth. Presenting her as a proactive anti-censorship campaigner, a headstrong libertine, shrewdly manipulating her own wanderings through the sex industry, the book over-compensates for what must have been quite the opposite. In reality, Mary was succumbing increasingly to irrationality and submissive promiscuity. She was, if anything, becoming more vulnerable, less able to sustain the Mary Millington image that had, after all, been created by a powerful man. One example: her autobiography quite ludicrously describes her hardcore porn films for John Lindsay as devices of her own making, things she instigated to support her ongoing fight for freedom of expression. But in reality, they are clearly the result of powers far beyond her control. Mary is almost invisible in them, a body for hire, as objectified as the women in

The Amazing
MARY
MILLINGTON
Mary Millington and David Weldon

a thousand stag films before and after. In fact, she is almost an irrelevance — disposable, manipulated and discarded at the climax.

In the last year of her life, another of Mary's chronic foibles — kleptomania — became more pronounced. A casual habit from her childhood days, her light shoplifting progressed to more criminal levels. She'd reportedly moved from knives and forks from the BBC canteen to expensive lamps and dresses from exclusive boutiques. In June 1979, Mary was arrested for shoplifting in a department store near her home in Surrey and a court appearance was scheduled for August 21.

In the meantime, the Inland Revenue decided to stick the boot in as well. Some months previously they had sent Mary a massive tax demand, which she resolutely refused to pay. Although it was a deliberately inflated figure and one that the Revenue could not have realistically expected full payment of, the shock of the amount sent Mary's stress levels through the roof. As she edged towards her thirty-fourth birthday, Mary could have been forgiven for thinking that the future held bankruptcy, the loss of her career and perhaps even prison.

On the morning of August 19,1979, Mary's long-suffering husband found her dead in her bed. She had taken an overdose of paracetamol tablets and washed them down with gin. The day before, she had been arrested again for stealing a necklace from a jeweller's shop in Banstead. When her husband had picked her up from the police station, she'd looked like a zombie.

Mary left suicide notes to several of her colleagues, friends and family. In one she wrote: "The police have framed me yet again. They frighten me so much. I can't face the thought of prison ... The Nazi tax man has finished me as well ..."

Mary had been lined up as the lead in Sullivan's next sex feature, *Emmanuelle in Soho*, which was eventually released "starring the new Mary Millington, 'Randy' Mandy Miller," in 1981. But where would Mary's career have gone after that? *Emmanuelle in Soho* was, effectively, the last theatrically released British soft porn film. Soon after, the new Conservative Government abolished the Eady Levy — a tax on theatre admissions that was channelled into domestic film production — thus severing a lifeline for British low budget cinema. At the same time, the rapid growth of the video market was closing cinemas up and down the country, making home-grown, exploitation film-making completely untenable. By then, Mary Millington would have been nudging thirty-six, yet she had done nothing on screen so far to suggest that she could have been anything else but a sex performer. It is very likely that, true to her worst fears, obscurity would have been waiting around the corner.

Twenty years after her death, cult fans eager to delve deeper into seventies sleaze made Mary a minor celebrity again. Websites, a biography and a TV documentary all revisited her life. She was a bona fide victim now. Wasted and abused, she was our own peroxide tart with a heart, a tap-room Marilyn Monroe. Her films will never stand up, but her life story is a cautionary tale with a timeless significance.

[Mary Millington filmography p.143]

MARY MILLINGTON as we knew her –
a smiling happy person who was
a great tonic to us all.

A SAD LOSS TO
US ALL

We write this editorial with great regret. The bullying tactics of certain police officers and tax inspectors clearly drove one of the nicest and most beautiful people to walk this earth to suicide. As a tribute to Mary Millington we publish extracts from her death bed letters which clearly leave no doubt about the reasons for her death:

1. Her letter to David Sullivan –
Dearest Dave,
The police have framed me yet again. They frightened me so much I can't face the thought of prison. They said I'll definitely go to Holloway and told me how bad it is there. I do hope porn is legal one day, they called me obscene names for being in possession of it and I can't go through any more with that Scotland Yard Porn Squad. I don't know how they can torment me all the time when there's so much violence in this world. I told them it was legal in virtually every country now and I wouldn't be in business if there wasn't such a great demand.
The Nazi Tax men have finished me as well. Please print in your magazines how much I want porn legalised, but the police have beaten me. I do hope you are luckier. All love Mary.

2. Extracts of a letter to her solicitor Michael Kaye –
The police have killed me with their threats. I want to be buried in my mothers grave at Holmwood with my mother. The police have made my life a misery with frame ups. All my money I leave to my dogs and the Battersea Dogs Home. The tax man has hounded me so much – I will be made bankrupt, he mustn't get anything of his £200,000 demands. He is a religious maniac and this is why he has hounded me. Pornography will be legal one day here as it is in most countries, but the abuse I

Publisher and Editor: Bill Edwards.

All rights reserved and reproductions without permission strictly forbidden. All contributions including colour transparencies and photographs submitted are sent at owner's risk and while every care is taken no responsibility can be assumed for loss or damage. All characters and events in this magazine are fictional unless specifically stated otherwise. The views and opinions of the contributors are not necessarily those of the publishers. Photographs used in this magazine were posed for by professional models and so are not intended to depict the real-life character or behaviour of the models. All letters and unsolicited material sent to this magazine will be assumed intended for publication and may be used for this purpose. An SAE must accompany any unsolicited material if return is required and this magazine cannot accept responsibility for loss or damage of such material.
The Publishers would like to state that all the photographs in this magazine feature simulated, not real sex and additionally, all the models are over 18 years of age and that all the captions attached to pictures in no way relate to the models who are all professional models.

receive from the police is unbearable. The police have threatened me so much I can't face the thought of Holloway where they're determined to get me. I wish for proceedings to continue against the 'detective' who beat me up.
Love to Bob, Trev, Auntie Eileen, Uncle Ted, John Emy, Teddy, Dave Sullivan, Dave Cash, Clayton, Sue Black, Sandra, all my love to all animals (especially my darling dogs Reject and Tippi) and all my readers.

It is a sad day for Britain when such a lovely person is driven to suicide by the acts of certain sections of our police force and tax department.
CAN WE ASK YOU ALL NOT to let Mary die in vain PLEASE write a letter about the way she has been treated to your M.P. who can be contacted at the House of Commons, London S.W.1 – please ask him to fulfill Mary's dying wish to LEGALISE pornography in Britain.

*Mary's obituary as it appeared in **Private** magazine, undated.*

Part 2: Tragic Comics

Tony Hancock
Down and Under

Tony Hancock's decline and fall is probably one of the best known stories in British celebrity folklore. In 1960, he was easily the most successful British comedian ever to have worked in radio and television, and the measure of his affection extended to millions of people, not just in Britain, but around the world. His BBC television show, which ran from 1956–61, was such a cherished national event that British streets were deserted when it was broadcast. And the show topped the ratings in Canada, New Zealand, South Africa and Australia. Every English-speaking nation had taken Hancock — the rankled, grimacing Everyman railing against the petty inconveniences of modern living — to their hearts. That is, every English-speaking nation except America.

Being as stubborn, insecure and, increasingly, egomaniacal as he was, Hancock was most displeased with his failure to gain recognition in the States, and from 1960 embarked on a ruthless strategy aimed at cracking that Golden Egg. After all, other comics had done it (Chaplin, Stan Laurel). Others were in the process of doing it (Peter Sellers, Terry-Thomas). And, some time in the future, others would do it (Dudley Moore, Benny Hill). What Hancock didn't seem to accept was that his much-loved persona was steeped in the parochialism of working/lower middle class England, whereas these successful rivals had either Americanised themselves or presented a guffawing, stereotypical Englishness that US audiences could laugh at. Nevertheless, Hancock believed he could change and broaden his appeal. And he was prepared to sacrifice anything to do it.

In a move to succeed on his own, Hancock ditched his agent, his solid co-star Sid James and his entire company of supporting character actors. He enlisted his long-time — and highly esteemed — writing team of Ray Galton and Alan Simpson to come up with a film that would establish him as a performer of universal appeal. They duly wrote *The Rebel* (1960). It wasn't a bad movie, and quite a lot of people liked it. In America, they hated it.

Hancock's final sitcom series for the BBC in 1961, however, was proof-positive to the increasingly megalomanic star that he could succeed on his own. As a solo performer, he carried the classic episodes of this series, which included 'The Blood Donor,' 'The Lift' and 'The Radio Ham,' into British television history. They are still regarded as yardsticks of television comedy, sublime scriptwriting and razor-edged timing, and their popular and critical success seemed at the time to be a valediction of Hancock's single-mindedness. And, as childish and self-absorbed as Hancock could be, this success went straight to his head. It was at this point that he decided he didn't need his writers either.

Ray Galton and Alan Simpson had written for Hancock since the early days of his radio career, and they were undoubtedly as responsible for the success of his comic persona as Hancock himself. Everyone but Hancock appreciated this. When he pushed Galton and Simpson out of the picture, Hancock foundered badly. His next film project, *The Punch and Judy Man* (1962) was overseen by Hancock himself, and co-written with a new collaborator. For a comedy film, it was uncomfortably mournful and melancholic; Hancock, in truly deluded style, defended this by saying that it wasn't supposed to be funny. Not surprisingly, *The Punch and Judy Man* managed to alienate even his British fans, and the rest of the pictures in his film contract were cancelled.

Hancock's rage to succeed and blinkered denial of his own artistic misjudgements was by this time being exacerbated by his chronic alcoholism, which had grown steadily worse during his years of success. Such was the saturating effect of his drinking, his wife Cicely had also become an alcoholic by trying to keep up with her husband to reduce his intake. Hancock nevertheless embarked on a thirteen-part sitcom, *Hancock*, for the rival British television channel, ITV, in 1963. Its ratings were patchy, not totally disastrous, but the show was a pale shadow of its predecessor. No second series was forthcoming.

Hancock spent 1964 embroiled in respective bouts of binge drinking and torturous detoxification, violent marital outbursts, and sporadic work for theatre and television. He began living more openly with his mistress, Freddie. And he was fast developing a reputation for being difficult to work with. But he was no less well loved by the British public, and the following year saw an offer he couldn't refuse — a part in a Hollywood Disney film, *The Adventures of Bullwhip Griffin*.

From the outset, however, Hancock failed to play the Hollywood game. Whereas most actors discreetly hide themselves away to learn their lines, a dishevelled Hancock would mutter them obsessively while guzzling champagne by the side of his hotel pool, making "the people around him feel uneasy". He grew bored with the slow process of Hollywood film-making, and began to spend time with the wife of another actor holed up in the Beverly Wilshire. True to form, this little liaison soon became too intense for the actress's taste, and Hancock ended up humiliating himself.

The comic certainly did not ingratiate himself with the Hollywood executive elite by wandering about "unshaven, red-eyed and crumpled". He then put the final nail in the coffin when he collapsed during filming. Already suspicious of his behaviour, the studio replaced Hancock while he was recovering in hospital. His Hollywood sojourn was over.

In 1966, Hancock tried to bury the hatchet with Galton and Simpson when he accepted a role in a proposed stage musical they had co-written, *Noah*. But the project was doomed from the start, with the exorbitant costs precluding such a volatile star. Nevertheless, Hancock remained almost pathologically deluded about the show's potential, and went on planning for it long after everyone had given up on it. At the same time, his second marriage (to Freddie) had hit the rocks almost immediately. Freddie Hancock later confessed to five suicide attempts while she was with the comedian. (One failed attempt, where she downed a handful of laxatives she had mistaken for barbiturates, amused the callous comic no end when he later regaled the tale.)

In September 1966, Hancock performed a one-man show at the Royal Festival Hall. Beforehand, he appealed to Ray Galton and Alan Simpson for new material, but they turned him down. Instead, he dusted off his trusted arsenal of hoary old chestnuts, and gave a creaky performance, which nevertheless seemed to impress the live audience. More discerning critics were nonetheless aghast. Freddie Hancock wrote: "It was a travesty of what Hancock had once been." His wife also noted that the drinking and the brutal attempts to stop drinking were also robbing Hancock of his truest gift — his timing. By the end of the year, their seven-month marriage was at an end.

But the public were still desperate for Hancock to regain his crown as the king of British comedy, and his Festival Hall performance and previous involvement with a variety series called *The Blackpool Show* led to the commissioning of his final series for British television, *Hancock's*, in 1967. Here he was the manager of a "swinging London nightclub", which gave him the opportunity to deliver a bit of ropey spiel and introduce a variety of guests. But Hancock, who had given up learning lines after the autocued success of 'The Blood Donor' six years earlier, was now so reliant on teleprompters that he looked about as animated as a Thunderbird puppet. This was when he actually could see the prompters, his vision being almost permanently clouded by an alcoholic haze. Aged forty-three, he looked at least ten years older. *Hancock's* was not a success, and lasted all of six episodes.

That same year, Hancock was invited by the promoter John Collins to take his live show to Australia, where he was revered with as much passion as in Britain. This turned out to be a pretty ominous experience, as one night the comic was so paralytic he ended up crawling over the stage on all fours. He then insulted the enraged audience by turning the spotlights on them, and was booed mercilessly as he was carried out of the theatre. Despite this debacle, Hancock gave the same audience a free show the next day, with the opening gambit, "As I was saying before I fell off the stage ..." The Ozzies must be a pretty forgiving bunch, because they lapped it up and the comic was immediately reinstated to his exalted position in their hearts.

Collins, a shrewd character to say the least, was clearly impressed by Hancock's redemptive powers, and in March 1968, brought the comic back

Tony Hancock

to Australia to star in a new television show for the Seven Network (ATN-7). Hancock had little choice but to accept. As the Australian show's director Edward Joffe said: "Nobody in the UK wanted to work with him. One day he would expose his soul in a flood of alcohol-induced emotion, the next he'd disappear into his private clam shell, broody, sullen, aloof and withdrawn, as difficult to approach as an electrified fence."

ATN-7 were nevertheless pinning a lot of hope onto this series. It was to be shot on 35mm film, in colour, for potential international sale. As such, it was the most expensive project they had ever undertaken. Yet when their star turned up he was a physical and emotional wreck. He'd weathered fifteen detoxification attempts in the past few years, was clearly unbalanced psychologically, and was now involved in a seemingly destructive, although admittedly passionate, affair with Joan Le Mesurier, the wife of actor John, one of his best friends.

Despite the fact that he was again off the wagon, and had to be entertained like a child with attention-deficit disorder when he wasn't working, Hancock was on good form at the first read-through of the first episode to be filmed. Consequently, an air of exhilaration filled the ATN-7 studio after the day's work. But by the end of the week, during rehearsal, a production assistant noticed that Hancock had to be cajoled into "uttering a few slurred lines of

Tony Hancock. **Hancock's Half Hour**

the script". A few days later, she commented: "Now he is just a pathetic, mumbling, red-eyed person who has to be led, coaxed and pushed through any scene he performs."

Within weeks, with rehearsals and filming descending into a daily catastrophe, producer-director Joffe appealed to the network to cancel the series. The first completed episode had to be scrapped. At the end of April 1968, the chairman of ATN-7 instead allowed Hancock a drying-out period, warning him "One more drink mate, and you're on the first plane back to Blighty."

For three weeks, Hancock went cold turkey in a clinic and then returned to filming the series. Struggling with sobriety, he managed to get two and a half episodes in the can, material that was competent at best. But other things apart from the absence of drink were plaguing Hancock by now. He was brooding darkly over the impasse in his relationship with Joan Le Mesurier, much of which stemmed from the sluggish postal system between the UK and Australia. His new digs hadn't yet received a phone, and he had been used to long, bank-breaking calls to his mother in the UK. Such inconveniences would be nothing more than a mild nuisance to a stable person, but Hancock was emotionally dependent on soothing words from the women in his life, and any day without contact was a nightmare for him. He was also dependent on drugs as a means to alleviate his black moods and depression: amphetamines and barbiturates made up just part of his daily pill-popping.

On the evening of June 24, 1968, Hancock found that he couldn't rehearse his lines in the usual way because his personal tape recorder had broken and he couldn't fix it. He couldn't find anybody to help, and began to worry about screwing up the next day's filming. Some say he had a moment of clarity that night, and saw what his life had really become. The horror of it must have appalled him. He was losing his talent and he had lost his best friends and collaborators. He was thousands of miles from home, making a series that looked patchy at best. He knew he didn't have the stamina to film the remaining twenty-three episodes that were mooted. On the back two pages of the script he was trying to learn, Hancock scrawled two suicide notes and washed down a large handful of amylo-barbitone tablets with a bottle of vodka. The next day, his director found him dead. Hancock was forty-four.

The completed episodes from the new series were cobbled together with new footage and shown on Australian TV as a 'special' some years after Hancock's death. It was never broadcast anywhere else.

[*Tony Hancock filmography p.143*]

Richard Beckinsale
The Dark Light Comedian

There was a point in the seventies, on British television, when the two great-est sitcoms of the decade were shown on the same night, albeit on different channels. And Richard Beckinsale was in both of them. Highly regarded when they were transmitted, both *Rising Damp* (ITV 1974–78) and *Porridge* (BBC TV 1974–77) have now achieved the kind of status usually reserved for prestigious drama. The writing and acting of both was of a quality rarely achieved in British situation comedies since.

Both series were propelled by powerhouse leading performances. Ronnie Barker in *Porridge* and Leonard Rossiter in *Rising Damp* both transcended the mantel of 'TV comedian' and played their roles with such sublime sub-tlety, focused energy and precise timing that they now stand as high points of television comedy acting. But both performances also needed strong sup-port to achieve a balance and work to their best advantage. This is where Beckinsale came in.

Although it may not have been totally appreciated at the time, to share the screen and feed and bounce off these comic perfectionists required a performance of almost equal skill. Richard Beckinsale, as the wide-eyed in-nocent — gullible, boyish and helplessly honest, deferring to and sparring with these middle-aged scenery-chewers — provided this comic balance with a deft blend of understated delivery and endearing vulnerability. Attractive, sincere and naive, Beckinsale became the nation's favourite son-in-law; he was the cherishably ordinary centre to two worlds of comic intensity.

Beckinsale had made his mark before *Porridge* and *Rising Damp*, however, as one of *The Lovers* (ITV 1970–71), in which he spent two series making faltering steps through a courtship with Paula Wilcox, trying awkwardly to get into her knickers, yet quite unsure of what he might find in there. He was an instant hit: the kind of guy girls wanted to be with, guys wanted to be mates with, and women wanted to mother. With his face locked in befuddled sexual confusion and his penchant for harmless outbursts of frustration, he personified a generation of provincial young men caught up in the throes of a 'permissive revolution' they could neither truly find nor really understand.

But there were more strings to Richard's bow than the 'naïve young man'; sadly, his brief career did not give him the opportunity to show them. Leav-ing school at fifteen, he worked as an upholsterer, a gas board clerk and, of all things, an inspector of iron piping before attempting to get into acting. He made it to RADA, and in the late sixties got a professional grounding at Crewe rep and spent time touring in provincial theatre productions. During his years of television success, he often returned to the stage, notably in a suc-

L–R   *Don Warrington, Richard Beckinsale,*
Leonard Rossiter. **Rising Damp**

cessful run of the sex comedy *Funny Peculiar*, in which he played a 'promiscuous north country grocer'. But it was on television that he was beginning to prove himself as a versatile straight actor, in director Stephen Frears' *Last Summer* (1976). By the time he was thirty, Beckinsale was eager to move away from his public image as the lovable boy-man.

But there were signs that the strain of overwork was already getting to him, and the need to project his darker feelings and fears was becoming stronger. He ducked out of the final series of *Rising Damp* in 1978 to take six months off. An actor friend, David Bradley, remembers holidaying with Beckinsale with their partners in Corfu around this time, and seeing the actor wake up one night, sweating in panic over fears of his mortality. Beckinsale's wife Judy Loe has since told how her husband was often stricken with panic attacks and a morbid fear of death. His casual jottings and poems, published by his wife in 1980, often betray a melancholy streak, speaking of inner pain and anticipating death. In one short piece, Beckinsale admits that "I am trying so desperately in my lifetime to find complete peace... But I have not yet retained or maintained a core of peaceful, tranquil strength through any of the pressures I have been under."

When he returned to work in late 1978, Beckinsale began to try and steer his career in a more mature and 'serious' direction. Aside from an obligatory big screen version of *Porridge* (1979), he accepted a crew-cutted, unsympathetic role, again for Stephen Frears, in the brutal television film *Red Saturday*, later released as *Bloody Kids* (1979). He also returned to the TV sitcom, but *Bloomers* (BBC TV 1979), written by playwright James Saunders, was a progression for the genre, dealing as it did more frankly with the sex life of an out-of-work actor.

Frears remembers lunching with Beckinsale during the *Bloody Kids* shoot. Beckinsale talked of his high cholesterol, before becoming angry that

Beckinsale and
Ronnie Barker.
Porridge

he wasn't being offered roles at the National Theatre. "Underneath it all, he had much more serious things going on," the director commented. "And he was just beginning to express them."

But Richard Beckinsale never got to fulfil his maturing talent. Having shot only a few scenes for *Bloody Kids*, and recorded five of the six episodes of *Bloomers*, he died from a massive heart attack on March 17, 1979. He was thirty-one.

The incomplete series of *Bloomers* was later transmitted, but there wasn't enough of Beckinsale in *Bloody Kids* to make the final cut. Had he lived, the actor would have undoubtedly branched out into more challenging and substantial roles in the 1980s. As it was, he was to be forever remembered, and cherished, as a fresh-faced comic foil.

Both Beckinsale's daughters later became actors. Samantha, a mirror image of her father, turns up sporadically on television. Oxford-educated Kate, only five at the time of his death, has easily eclipsed him in terms of a film career, landing leading roles in *The Last Days of Disco* (1998) and *Pearl Harbor* (2001). But, in Britain, the affection that endures for Richard Beckinsale still overshadows the success of his talented offspring.

[*Richard Beckinsale filmography p.144*]

Peter Sellers

Curse of the Pink Panther

In 1974, Peter Sellers' career was at such a low ebb that he agreed to offer his services for a television show. He had appeared on television specials throughout his stardom, of course, but featuring regularly in a series was something he hadn't done since the by-*Goon* days of the mid-fifties, when he appeared with Spike Milligan *et al* in *The Idiot Weekly, Price 2d* and its hasty successors *A Show Called Fred* and *Son of Fred*. But recently his association with a string of film flops — dating roughly from the time of his first major heart attack in 1964 — had lowered his stock. Once commanding $1m a picture, Sellers was now offering himself for $100,000 plus ten percent of the gross — and the gross, invariably, wasn't much, given that his films were sinking without trace at the box office. *Casino Royale* (1967), *The Bobo* (1967), *Hoffman* (1969), *There's A Girl in My Soup* (1970), *Soft Beds, Hard Battles* (1973), *Ghost in the Noonday Sun* (1973), *The Blockhouse* (1974) — all had been critical and commercial disasters. The last two were not even released.

But salvation came with Lew Grade, who was never short of commercial ideas, even if they were for television. And Grade had the money to lure the stars. He already had Roger Moore and Tony Curtis in his stable; he produced variety specials for Tom Jones and Julie Andrews. And now he had Andrews' husband, filmmaker Blake Edwards — also at a professional low point — on board too.

The new project was *The Return of the Pink Panther*, which would reunite Sellers and Edwards, revive the bumbling Inspector Clouseau (last played by Sellers in *A Shot in the Dark* ten years earlier) and package the whole thing for international TV syndication.

But as Edwards developed the script, he saw potential for something bigger than a TV series. Embellishing the thin story with broad jokes and pyrotechnical slapstick, the director pressured Grade to hike the project up to big screen level. Grade acquiesced when Edwards promised that he and Sellers would defer their salaries for a percentage of the box office gross. Sellers — co-operative as he was at such low points — went along. And *The Return of the Pink Panther* went through the roof.

Costing $3 million, *Return* made $33 million on its initial release. In today's money, it would be a hundred-million-dollar picture. As a 1975 release, only *Jaws* overshadowed it at the box office. Overnight, the film revived Sellers' and Edwards' careers, thrusting them back into the commercial A-list and going some way to consolidating their wealth for the rest of their lives. And for Sellers, it refuelled the awesome power he had wielded at the height of the

Peter Sellers

sixties. For his career, this was a lifesaver. But for his physical and mental health, and for those around him, it was something of a poisoned chalice.

Sellers had almost died ten years before, when, on arriving in Hollywood to make his first American film, he suffered eight consecutive heart attacks in one night. At the hospital, he was, he later claimed, pronounced clinically dead for two minutes. The actor seemed to recover physically, but mentally this morbid episode was something of a turning point. Whatever paranoia, egomania and cruelty he had displayed in his early career seemed to intensify with the near-death experience. From this point on, Sellers became more scared of losing control, more susceptible to outbursts of juvenile vitriol, and more reliant on the macabre guidance of superstition and the paranormal. On set, he could be more of a monster: unprofessional, childish, sullen, unco-operative. He threw tantrums, harboured cold rages, threatened to close down films and thought little of ruining careers. So when *The Return of the Pink Panther* and its hurried sequel, *The Pink Panther Strikes Again* (1976) put him back on top, it was open season again on anyone who got in his way.

With three failed marriages behind him, Sellers was now romantically

Peter Sellers and Lynne Frederick.

involved with a twenty-two-year-old actress called Lynne Frederick. And although he was nearly thirty years her senior, Sellers was no more mature. Indeed, he was still in the shadow of his late, over-protective mother — no woman could indulge him the way she had. But where he'd always craved love and affection, he now also needed care. From the mid-seventies, Sellers' fractious health had begun to deteriorate significantly. His heart had held up for ten years but now it was showing sings of giving in. He considered having a bypass operation in 1976 (set to be performed by his friend, the legendary heart surgeon Christiaan Barnard in South Africa), but got cold feet at the last minute and scrambled home before he could be talked round. He chose instead to rely on the intensive care of his new trophy girlfriend.

Lynne Frederick was a modestly successful actress — she'd been in films for seven or eight years. She quit school at fifteen and appeared in Cornel Wilde's torpid eco-drama *No Blade of Grass* (1970). From then on she was kept fairly busy as a child-woman in supporting roles throughout the early seventies: *The Amazing Mr. Blunden* (1972), *Vampire Circus* (1972), *The Six Wives of Henry VIII* (1972), *Phase IV* (1973) and *Voyage of the Damned* (1976).

Her first leading role, however, was more downmarket. In the hysterical Peter Walker horror thriller, *Schizo* (1976), she was required to do little more than scream and show her breasts. Although time was on her side, she was clearly light years away from scaling the artistic heights once known by her superstar boyfriend.

So Lynne Frederick went from appearing in *Schizo* to marrying one. She could, at least, have been forgiven for later thinking that. When the couple tied the knot in February 1977, Sellers was an emotional and physical time bomb. Predictably, within weeks of marrying her, her emotional destruction began.

Roger Lewis, in his controversial biography of Sellers, claims that the actor's relationship with Lynne "oscillated from ardour to hatred, reconciliation and remorse ... Of all of his wives, she had the most terrible time." This terrible time manifested itself in an emotional boxing match between the heavyweight Sellers and the featherweight Lynne. Or rather, Lynne became the punching bag. Sellers would send her a telegram stating "It's over," and then follow it with a bouquet of flowers and a note saying, "I didn't mean it." He would accuse her of having affairs with men she'd only just met. He would cut her out of his will, and then put her back in. Yet his mental and physical deterioration elicited her sympathy — the devoted Lynne continued to play his nursemaid, his valet, his co-star and his mother.

Lynne's career as a performer, however, immediately took second place as Sellers' heart scares started to occur more frequently. Just a month after the couple were married, in March 1977, the actor was taken ill on a flight from Paris to London. The heart attack was publicly put down to a bad batch of oysters — Sellers could not afford to advertise his ailing health and thus jeopardise his revived superstardom. Nevertheless, he had to have a pacemaker installed; weeks later, he was back in hospital when this broke down. Then the new one went awry. In May, the star was rushed to hospital again when the wire broke on his third pacemaker. Despite all these health setbacks, he signed up for his fifth *Pink Panther* film.

In *Revenge of the Pink Panther* (1978), however, the strain showed. Not just in Sellers' performance, but in the tired pace of the project. Where *The Return of the Pink Panther* and *The Pink Panther Strikes Again* had been humorous and endearing, *Revenge* was a laboured, stunt-heavy hotchpotch of half-baked ideas and rehashed gags. Despite the elaborate destruction of the set pieces, it pretty much failed to sustain one decent moment of comedy. And Sellers only really appears in half the movie. As is well-documented, the emphasis on knockabout routines and sub-Tatiesque pratfalling necessitated a reliance on stunt

"THE BRIGHTEST COMEDY THIS YEAR!"
—N.Y. TIMES

'I'M ALL RIGHT JACK'

Starring
PETER SELLERS · IAN CARMICHAEL
TERRY-THOMAS · A BOULTING BROTHERS PRODUCTION A COLUMBIA PICTURES RELEASE

doubles and stand-ins — so if it is Sellers you see in the close-up, more often than not, it's someone else in the medium and long shots. (There is little wonder that Blake Edwards could go on to make a Clouseau film without Sellers' direct involvement at all, as he did two years after the actor's death with *Trail of the Pink Panther*. *Trail* was assembled from outtakes of Sellers and new scenes of stand-ins. Edwards could probably have made another two or three *Panther* movies this way.)

Even so, with a high profile campaign behind it, *Revenge* did very respectable business — it grossed more money than the last two. Such commercial success instantly green-lighted a sixth film in the series.

By now, though, Sellers had driven Blake Edwards to snapping point. "With each film, Sellers co-operated less and less and got stranger and madder," Edwards later claimed. "And the sicker he got — and his illness had a lot to do with it — the less able he was to function... If you gave him any kind of physical moves in scenes in which he also had lines, he became literally incapable of doing both..." But if Edwards retained some sympathy for Sellers' ailing health, he had none for his deliberately destructive behaviour. After *Revenge*, the two vowed never to work with one another again. Edwards was paid off, and left the series (albeit temporarily, as it turned out).

In the meantime, there were different movies to make. Sellers signed a three-picture deal with producer Walter Mirisch. The first of these, he decided, was to be (yet another) remake of *The Prisoner of Zenda*. Playing two roles (Cockney cab driver Sid Frewin and his Royal Ruritanian doppelganger King Rudolph) Sellers wreaked the usual havoc on the set. Directors were sacked, the film went over-budget and over-schedule. And the result was uninspired, flat and almost utterly unfunny. Indeed, *The Prisoner of Zenda* (1979) might have passed almost entirely without notice, had its star decided not to publicly attack it before it was even released. Sellers poisoned the whole project when, in an on-the-record conversation with journalist Roderick Mann, he advised people *not* to go and see the film. He clearly cannot have had much concern for Lynne Frederick's career at this point — she had starred alongside him. Walter Mirisch was horrified. He cancelled the remaining two films in Seller's contract and declared he wanted nothing to do with the star ever again.

Personally and professionally, Sellers seemed to be on the slide again, despite the material riches that the *Pink Panthers* were bringing. He was unable to recapture the

15-year-old Lynne Frederick, who makes her acting debut as Mary in MGM's "No Blade of Grass," finds little comfort in Roger played by John Hamill, after being raped by a group of outlaw motor-cyclists. The film, by producer/director Cornel Wilde, is a study in environmental pollution.   2C

L–R   Harry Secombe, Michael Bentine, Peter Sellers, Spike Milligen. The Goons.

sometimes astounding inventiveness of his pre-1964 roles: *The Naked Truth* (1957), *I'm All Right Jack* (1959), *Only Two Can Play* (1962) and his two triumphs for Stanley Kubrick: *Lolita* (1962) and *Dr Strangelove* (1963). Even his performances as Clouseau — funny as they were — lacked some of the deft timing and comic nuance of his first two outings as the character, in *The Pink Panther* (1963) and *A Shot in the Dark* (1964). The Clouseau of the seventies had become the cartoon character of the animated *Pink Panther* TV series, crashing headlong through windows and doors, being blown up by hand-delivered bombs and spouting a French accent so over-the-top that none of the other characters in the films could understand what he was saying.

But if any comic actor of his generation could have truly merited the description 'genius', it was still probably Sellers. Spike Milligan, however, may have put it best when he claimed that Sellers wasn't a genius, he was a freak. (It was an offbeat compliment.) Sellers' freak talent could see his creative powers run amok — he often improvised in kind of a trance, as if it was the result of some bizarre fusion of method acting and self-hypnosis. He thus created 'genius' performances almost out of nowhere, just by donning a moustache or a uniform or a pair of glasses and falling into character. And although this talent was now impaired by his failing health and his growing wealth and status, it hadn't fallen dormant completely. There were still great Sellers moments in the later films: *What's New Pussycat?* (1965), *The Party* (1968), *Alice's Adventures in Wonderland* (1972) and *The Optimists of Nine Elms* (1973). Similarly, there were moments of sublime buffoonery in the new *Panthers*, *Murder by Death* (1976) and even *The Fiendish Plot of Dr*

Sellers in his most famous persona,
Inspector Clouseau.

Fu Manchu (1980). The sad thing was that Sellers' control of his talent had faltered — growing patches of laziness and narcissistic indulgence were staining what had once been a blanket of comic perfection.

Nevertheless, one important door had been opened by the commercial success of the new *Panther* movies. Somehow, Sellers seemed to be willing himself to live long enough to make *Being There* (1979). But even this was touch and go. In December 1978, just before shooting was to begin, he was taken ill with severe heart pains on another flight (this time it was New York to Geneva). The esteemed Alexander Walker, another Sellers biographer, points out, however, that "[f]ortunately, Peter had passed the medical for his *Being There* insurance cover only a few days earlier."

It was indeed fortunate. As many critics have pointed out, *Being There* would have stood as a worthy epitaph to the actor's career, had it been his last film. Certainly, it offered Sellers the opportunity to 'act', to immerse himself in the construction of an offbeat character, and to draw upon his powers of invention for the first time in years. (Ironically, the character of Chance — a mentally deficient gardener who stumbles into the Washington corridors of power and is taken for a political genius — is resolutely one-dimensional. Chance speaks and moves slowly, his face is blank, and he has no understanding of the world around him.) And Sellers knew that, after almost a decade of trying to put the film together (he had first read — and fell in love with — Jerzy Kosinki's novella in 1971), this was his last challenge, his last chance to prove something.

With its funereal quietness, autumnal grace and restrained comedy, *Being There* is a touching swan song. Yet there is also a despairing sobriety to it, and it is long and draining. And, more disturbingly, it can sometimes be difficult to tell whether there actually is an acting genius at work here: one could be forgiven for seeing a pronounced weariness in Sellers' low key performance as Chance, an involuntary sadness. Although the film revolves around him, much of the acting weight is shouldered by Melvyn Douglas and Shirley Maclaine (both of whom are excellent).

Nevertheless, *Being There* brought Sellers some of the artistic credibility he had been yearning for — he was nominated for an Oscar, feted at Cannes, and given a pat on the back by the critics who'd been growing more and more exasperated with his films for the last fifteen years.

But now that his last ambition had been realised, Sellers' life wish diminished dramatically. After *Being There*, his physical and mental deterioration became rapid. And his marriage to Lynne Frederick hit crisis point. In early 1979, the star confessed to David Lewin of the *Daily Mail*: "My marriage is over. We thought it would last forever. But few things do." Soon after, in July, the couple signed a separation agreement. By that time, they had been living apart for some months — Lynne in Los Angeles, Sellers in his tax haven chalet in Gstaad. Characteristically, Sellers struck Lynne from his will, pledging instead to leave his entire estate to the British Heart Foundation (once again ignoring his three children).

Sellers' son Michael has said that, at this point, "we all thought how ill he looked and he expressed the most alarming fear to Mum that he might have suffered brain damage on the first series of his heart attacks. Now a sad figure, it was if he had nothing in his life at all. A millionaire with nothing. And no-one. Even the clown within him had gone." Sellers had also fallen impotent, which had placed another frustrating strain on his failing marriage. But with this powerlessness overwhelming him, the actor decided he couldn't lose his nursemaid wife. Just as he was scheduled to sign the final divorce papers, he implored Lynne to give the marriage another chance. She acquiesced, although on some strict financial terms. A codicil to Sellers' will, made in October 1979, reinstated her as the main beneficiary.

Sellers was now setting up films simply to keep himself alive. *The Fiendish Plot of Dr Fu Manchu* (1980) with its lame, *Prisoner of Zenda*, dual-role hysterics, was another of these vanity projects, and served little other purpose than for the actor to surround himself with old friends and sycophants and to misbehave on a spectacular scale. By the time *Fu Manchu* started shooting, in late 1979, Sellers had nothing left to prove. So he crapped all over the

Clouseau (Sellers) gets the upperhand on Cato (Bert Kwouk).

Lynne Frederick. **Schizo**

film — firing the crew left, right and centre, assuming control of the direction, installing a redundant Lynne as a production executive, causing chaos to the production schedule and generally behaving like a spoilt child. And the alarming change in his physical appearance was now on show for all to see: the well-fed, bright-eyed fifty-something of *Being There* had given way to a tired, emaciated old man.

Once again, the film had to be delayed while Sellers recovered from heart trouble — again over Christmas. He completed *Fu Manchu*, but had to give up shooting a series of commercials for Barclay's Bank in Dublin in early 1980 when he suffered another heart scare. And once again, in order not to alarm the United Artists executives, who were earmarking him for the next *Pink Panther* romp, this news was played down.

One of these UA executives was Steven Bach, who later wrote *Final Cut*, the definitive account of the studio's eventual decline and fall in the wake of the *Heaven's Gate* fiasco. In June 1980, Bach was dispatched to Sellers' home in Gstaad to negotiate what was now known as *The Romance of the Pink Panther*. He was disturbed to find that Sellers was "wraithlike... His skull, his fingers, the tightly drawn, almost transparent skin — all seemed frail, infinitely fragile." Sellers was, Bach went on, "a spectral presence, a man made of eggshells." Even so, United Artists, desperate for something bankable, pressed on with the film, and shooting was scheduled to begin in August 1980 (Sellers had co-written the script himself — surely another recipe for disaster. Still, his fee for the picture was to be an unprecedented $3m plus a healthy percentage of the gross receipts — superstar earnings for sure). The actor was, nonetheless, more painfully aware than ever of his mortality and the inevitable battering his heart would take from another *Panther*. He decided, then, to finally override his fear of the surgeon's knife and submit to an angiogram, a surgical examination of the heart. The operation was set for late July.

Meanwhile, Sellers relationship with Lynne appeared to be breaking down again. Although they had tentatively reunited several months before, they had still endured periods of separation and acrimony. According to his son

Michael, Sellers was talking seriously about finalising the divorce again by this time.

But Sellers would not have time to see the divorce, or indeed the angiogram, through. On 22 July, he collapsed in his room at the Dorchester Hotel, London, having flown back into town for a reunion with fellow Goons Spike Milligan and Harry Secombe. Taken to Middlesex Hospital, he was kept alive for thirty-six hours, but this time the heart attack had been too damaging to repair. Sellers died on 24 July, 1980. He was fifty-four.

Disturbingly, Sellers' demise also set his widow on a long path to self-destruction. And perhaps something of the star's legendary selfishness and vindictiveness had rubbed off on Lynne Frederick. For her behaviour after his death was not in keeping with the coquettish, altruistic wife she had appeared to be at times during his final years.

Sellers had left Frederick, in his hastily revised will, almost everything (a reported four million pounds). To his three children he left the insulting sum of £750 each (a token amount that he had to set aside to prove that he hadn't inadvertently omitted them). The star would no doubt have changed this will had he lived a few more months. Indeed, he probably would have continued to change it according to his whim, which was apt to fluctuate from dewy-eyed affection to snarling dismissal on a daily basis. At any rate, any good person would have appreciated this, and at least attempted some compromise with his children after his death. Lynne Frederick didn't; she walked away from Sellers' funeral a multi-millionairess.

Exactly six months after Sellers' death, Lynne married the TV personality David Frost. This ended little more than a year later, after she miscarried their child. In January 1983, she married a Los Angeles heart specialist, Barry Unger, giving birth to their daughter in May. But she also split with him within a couple of years, although they didn't divorce until several years later. Reportedly, she had filled their marital home with photographs of Sellers, and had even devoted a room to his memory.

Throughout these marriages, and subsequently, Frederick played the star's grieving widow, always referring to herself as Mrs Sellers. In 1985, she famously sued United Artists for using footage of the actor in the aforementioned *Trail of the Pink Panther* (1982). Winning the lawsuit, she netted another million. Despite this, she claimed: "I hope this shows that I'm not a gold-digger. I've risked my entire fortune and the financial future of my daughter to protect Peter's reputation." In 1989, she stopped a film about the actor going into production because it was set to recreate scenes of the actor's death and funeral. She claimed that it was not enough of a tribute.

Cynics sneered at this, but the slow decline of Lynne Frederick over the next few years pointed to a genuinely self-destructive obsession with her former husband. Unable to erase the memory of Sellers, Frederick, now permanently residing in Los Angeles, began to fritter her fortune away on drugs and alcohol (£2500 a week on cocaine), destroying her looks by blowing up to 14 stone in the process. She reportedly turned her opulent home into a shrine to Sellers. She also seemed to be continuing the actor's meanness, as if living out his dying wish — denying his children access to a fair inheritance, even to family photographs of their father, and refusing to return comedy material to Spike Milligan. Roger Lewis concludes that "Lynne was, in a way [Sellers'] supernatural double or fellow lost soul; except that she acquired his insanities without the compensations of his genius."

But could one so callous have let herself go in quite such an undignified, pitiful manner? Could one so calculating, self-obsessed and single-minded have allowed herself to deteriorate — physically and mentally — in quite such a fashion? Maybe. But it was clear that something had haunted her final years. Something had transformed Lynne Frederick from an inoffensive actress to a friendless, bloated drug-addict. Was it the ghost of Peter Sellers? The Curse of the Pink Panther?

In the last year of her life, Lynne Frederick was quoted as saying of Sellers: "I am still hopelessly in love with him. No-one can replace him." On April 27, 1994, with a history of seizures and alcohol-related problems, she choked to death on a meal at her Los Angeles home. She was thirty-nine.

[*Peter Sellers filmography p.144*]

Charles Hawtrey
Sixteen Year Bender

The highs and lows of Charles Hawtrey's life and career are, on the surface, comparable to that of his *Carry On* colleague, Kenneth Williams. Both performers were, more so than Sid James, the true, long-serving comic staples of the entire *Carry On* series, from its gentle beginnings in the fifties to the smutty vulgarity of the seventies. (Hawtrey appeared in a whopping twenty-three *Carry On*s; Williams stayed around to make twenty-seven.) And offscreen, significantly, Hawtrey and Williams were unfulfilled, lonely men. They were both homosexual — albeit to very different degrees of practice — when it was much less acceptable to be so; both were rather fond of the sauce; both were given to wildly inappropriate behaviour in situations that demanded some social restraint; and, tragically, both were apparently imbued with a terminally self-destructive streak. And, in 1988, they died within six months of each other.

But it is where Hawtrey differs from Williams that is most revealing. Although they were accomplished comic performers with time-served apprenticeships in similar kinds of stage, screen and radio revues, and were both irrepressibly camp in almost everything that they did, Hawtrey's style could hardly have been more different from that of Williams. Where Williams

Charles Hawtry, early publicity shot.

was repressed, sarcastic and often piously self-contained, at least until his inevitably hysterical breaking point, Hawtrey was warm, earthy and sexually mischievous. Where Williams would spend an entire *Carry On* squirming and bristling like a trapped cat to escape the intoxicated love-grip of a frustrated Hattie Jacques, Hawtrey would more often than not gladly strip down to his boxer shorts and get pissed on brandy with her, giggling away coyly as he did so. Williams marches snootily about the screen, buttoned up to the throat in a conservative suit; Hawtrey minces around in an orange shirt and pink chiffon scarf. Williams looks down his nose at us. Hawtrey, instead, flirts

Hawtry carries on... with Sid James (top).

with us, looking directly at the camera with a little wink and a naughty smile.

But there were also marked differences in the offscreen personalities of Hawtrey and Williams, and these were the traits that truly affected their careers. For all his *ennui*, self-loathing and contempt for the material he was working with, Williams remained ensconced in the *Carry On* series until its demise in 1978, and he spent the rest of his career busy with the kind of voiceovers, radio appearances and one-man shows that he was already a veteran of. Something of a loose cannon, he was nonetheless always professional. Most significantly, he had always strenuously repressed his own transparent homosexuality, almost to the point of self-denial.

By contrast, Hawtrey was more dangerous and undisciplined in his later years. He became unreliable, was invariably drunk, and made no secret of his voracious urges — eyewitnesses observed him pitifully trying to seduce sailors in his local pubs, and Barbara Windsor recounted how he chased after George Best at a publicity event in Manchester. Perhaps not surprisingly, when Hawtrey finally fell out with the *Carry On* team in 1972, his career was harder to sustain.

There is a story that Hawtrey quit the *Carry On* series because the producer and director wouldn't let him have a star on his dressing room door. This incident did apparently occur, during the making of *Carry On Abroad* (1972), and the fact he was refused this minor indulgence is totally in keeping with the stern, humourless control that producer Peter Rogers and director Gerald Thomas exerted over their actors. But Hawtrey had already been burning his bridges with Rogers and Thomas for a number of years — by frequently turning up too drunk for work and squabbling over his billing. To their credit, Rogers and Thomas did seem to tolerate Hawtrey's bad behaviour for a while — they even cast him as a drunk in *Carry On Abroad* precisely because he was out of his head throughout the shoot. They also appreciated that Hawtrey was a key ingredient in the *Carry On* mix, and that they owed him more than they were perhaps prepared to admit.

The termination of Hawtrey's *Carry On* career actually occurred later in 1972, when he was to be involved in one of the team's regular *Carry On Christmas* television specials. With Sid James and Kenneth Williams not scheduled to appear, Hawtrey demanded top billing. But Gerald Thomas insisted that that honour was going to Hattie Jacques — not as long-serving a member of film series, but by then a television personality of higher standing. As Hawtrey had been written into the script of the special and had even been involved in

Carry On Spying

some advance publicity for it, Thomas was keen to retain his services, but persisted in offering the actor second billing. Hawtrey, in turn, persisted in refusing. Two days before the start of taping, Thomas telephoned Hawtrey (who was lunching, as usual, in a department store restaurant) and tried to secure his services one final time. Hawtrey still said no.

He might not have realised it straight away, but Hawtrey cut his last tie with this display of stubbornness. One thing that Rogers and Thomas never did was indulge their stars (or properly appreciate them, in many people's eyes) and they weren't about to be pushed around by Hawtrey with a tight TV schedule pressing. As Rogers himself commented: "There was no question Charles Hawtrey was going to hold me to ransom — no way we'd trust Charles Hawtrey after letting us down like that."

Hawtrey fell immediately, and somewhat deliberately, into the show business wilderness. The *Carry On* team had undoubtedly needed him, but Hawtrey had also needed *Carry On*, even more than Williams did (and much more so than an established TV star like Sid James) — for exposure, for money and, saddest of all, for company. Nevertheless, he was excluded from the further films in the series — *Carry On Girls* (1973); *Dick* (1974); *Behind* (1975); *England* (1976) and *Emmanuelle* (1978), even though all of them would

Hawtrey in his heyday.

have benefited immeasurably from his presence.

Despite having forty years experience in film and television comedy, Hawtrey retreated instead to panto and provincial summer seasons in which he toured the country in walk-on parts that capitalised on his familiar *Carry On* persona. But this work was infrequent, and Hawtrey was usually drunk when he did it. In reality, the ageing actor had opted to live modestly in retirement, which unfortunately freed up more time for his principal interests — drinking himself stupid and trying to get off with men barely out of their teens.

In the early seventies, Hawtrey went to live in the small town of Deal on the Kent coast, not least because it was populated by a bevy of handsome sailor boys. Whether he thought that this relocation would result in an endless stream of sexual conquests is unclear. At this time such openly gay behaviour would not have been particularly welcome in cosmopolitan cities, let alone small towns. What is well-known is that Hawtrey proceeded to make a first-class nuisance of himself around the town, particularly in its watering holes, where he frequently imbibed well beyond the capacity of his tiny frame, and was given to increasing displays of rudeness and lecherousness.

When not out raising hell in the pubs in Deal, Hawtrey spent his evenings ranting at his cat, which — according Roger Lewis' essay-biography of the star — was also something of an alcoholic, given that it was fed on a diet of "port-soaked sugar lumps and sherry-spiked butter". Lewis goes on to describe Hawtrey's own nightly diet as "two and a half bottles of port, a quantity of whiskey and a pot of tea". Hawtrey drunkenly shared both his high and low moods with his feline companion, either wistfully recounting anecdotes and stories to it, or screaming blue murder at it for ignoring him.

Hawtrey had always drunk to excess, but now he had nothing to sober up for. His days were wasting away in a blur of alcohol, regret and overt bitterness towards his former employers and colleagues. In 1979 he did manage a fleeting appearance as one of the many cameos in Eric Sykes' silent TV comedy, *The Plank*, but then he promptly disappeared from view again. When he next made a splash with the public, five years later, it was in far less agreeable circumstances.

In August 1984, Hawtrey's house caught fire when he left a cigarette burning on the sofa. The incident was fairly newsworthy, but it was made much more so by the fact that Charlie was naked when he was rescued from his bedroom, wherein, it transpired, a very young man (some reports say all of sixteen years old), with just his trousers on, was still trapped. The incident is comically recounted by Kenneth Williams in a subsequently published letter. "When safely down the ladder, a fireman assured Hawtrey, 'You're all right now.' Hawtrey replied, 'No, I'm not. My fags are upstairs by the bed, and my boyfriend's in it.'" In reality, the episode was an embarrassing one for Hawtrey, who was, moments after being rescued, snapped by a news photographer. He looked haggard, distressed and, most shockingly, pitifully naked without his clothes or his trademark black toupee. It was also an event that led to a degree of persecution in the subsequent months.

There is no way an old celebrity caught *in flagrante delicto* with a sixteen-year-old boy would emerge scott-free today, and it is amazing that Hawtrey wasn't dragged through the coals more severely in 1984, when the age of consent for homosexuality was still set solidly at twenty-one. Still, other reports have put the age of the young accomplice as 'early twenties' so this might have eased the onslaught. Either way, the incident soon faded into the tabloid ether. But Hawtrey had cooked his goose as far as some of his fellow Deal residents were concerned. As Lewis comments, the actor soon "became a target for lager louts, who shouted abuse through his letter-box". Sometimes too frightened to go out, Hawtrey would also "despatch a taxi to do his shopping …"

The next four years saw further decline in Hawtrey's health and mindset. One by one, he began to get barred from all the pubs in Deal, such was the nuisance he was making of himself. He alienated all his remaining acquaintances, and was indignant to many who simply wanted to seek him out and pay their respects. (He'd never had any close friends to speak of. His closest bond, somewhat predictably, had been with his mother.) When anyone asked him about the *Carry On* films, he launched into a tirade of resentment. By the mid eighties, half-hour compilation shows of the old films were being screened week after week on British TV, but Hawtrey and his fellow *Carry On* actors saw not a penny in residuals, all of which went to Rogers and Thomas.

Somehow, during this time, Hawtrey did manage to focus his vision long enough to get through an episode of the children's TV comedy *Supergran*, as a guest star (the show was transmitted in early 1987). This was his last ever screen role, and it seemed to come out of the blue — he'd been absent from film and TV for eight years. But it did not symbolise any kind of return to form. Hawtrey was in frail health by now. A series of heart scares in the mid eighties had put paid to resuming any kind of real career.

In October 1988, Hawtrey collapsed, drunk again, in the doorway of another Deal drinking establishment. In doing so, he badly broke one of his legs, but, when he got to the hospital, the doctors had graver concerns. The seventy-three year old star had serious circulatory problems brought on by years of heavy smoking. Hawtrey was told that he had to lose both legs if he was to live. Characteristically stubborn, he flatly refused to go through with the necessary double amputation. (Four years earlier, after the house fire, he had also refused hospital treatment for his burns, regarding himself as 'self-healing'.) He said he'd prefer to die with his boots on.

Hawtrey was transferred to a nursing home in Deal, where he spent his last days. He died on October 27, 1988. Nine people attended his funeral.

[*Charles Hawtrey filmography p.145*]

Benny Hill

The Show's Over

In June 1989, Benny Hill was summoned to a meeting with Thames TV's new Head of Light Entertainment, John Howard Davies. The comedian took his longtime friend and producer-director, Dennis Kirkland, along with him. They assumed the morning meeting was to be an informal discussion about the next series of *The Benny Hill Show*, which was still being produced, three times a year, by Thames, as it had been for twenty years. Hill and Kirkland liked to put on a bit of a comic act when out together, for their own and for others' amusement, and when called into Davies' office, they did a bit of Laurel and Hardy shtick at the doorway, bumping into each other, making a meal out of trying to get through it.

Davies quickly put an end to this hilarity by asking to see Benny alone. A few minutes later, Kirkland was called back in and saw Hill looking shaken. He had, effectively, been fired.

Since the early eighties, Benny Hill had come in for an increasing amount of criticism in Britain, from women's groups, from the National Viewers and Listeners Association and, perhaps most hurtfully, from the new generation of young, alternative comedians. Some of this was valid: his shows were increasingly out of step with modern sensibilities, the jokes were tired, arguable amounts of sexism and racism abounded, and, by the mid-eighties, the saucy postcard humour was almost embarrassingly anachronistic. None of these traits was unusual in comedy and variety shows ten years earlier, but the times were changing fast, and the other post-war comics who relied on this dated sort of material had all but vanished from British TV by 1984. Hill, however, had always been more talented than most of his contemporaries, and his infectious comic glint was still as strong as ever.

More damaging for Hill, though, was the marked 'sexing up' of the dances and sketches in his series — one controversial routine from an early eight-

Benny Hill

ies show had the cameraman zooming in slow motion into the crotch of a scantily-clad, cartwheeling dancer. It was *Electric Blue* with marginally more clothes. Understandably, some people watching at eight o' clock in the evening were moved to complain.

But throughout the first half of the eighties, it is fair to say, Hill had actually been encouraged to pull out the stops with regard to raunch and sauciness — by his director, Kirkland, and by the male-oriented tabloid newspapers that fed ravenously from his onscreen, and, increasingly, off-screen antics. And Hill had certainly not been dissuaded by the executives at Thames. They had been, until the appointment of John Howard Davies,

Benny as Ernie, the fastest milkman in the West.

understandably keen to keep Benny happy. He was, after all, their biggest global moneymaker

In 1979, in a historic piece of transatlantic television marketing, Thames' US agent Don Taffner launched a series of re-edited, half hour versions of Hill's Thames shows into American syndication. The Americans had seen nothing as 'naughty' on television before and were instantly hooked; by the end of the year, Benny Hill was a household name in the States. And, as his biographer Mark Lewisohn comments, "Once America was broken, the rest of the globe quickly followed."

But Benny Hill was a private, emotionally fragile and shy man, and he reacted to global success in the same way as he reacted to the increasing criticism at home — with some bewilderment and fear. A factor that must have niggled his rivals and contemporaries was that he'd never had any desire to crack America, and didn't even want to go there to visit when his success had reached stratospheric levels. Benny was much more content to stay in his rented flat and eat fish fingers. In 1984, however, he acquiesced, and went over to the US on a visit, whereupon he was greeted like some sort of comic messiah, with megastars such as Clint Eastwood, Burt Reynolds and Jack Lemmon clamouring to spend time with him.

Similarly, Hill eventually responded to the criticism at home. Towards the end of his series, he toned down his act, introducing Hill's Little Angels, a tribe of cute kids in front of whom he became Uncle Benny, a cuddly buffoon in a series of forgettable but harmless sketches. But this move was shutting the stable door after horse had bolted. Even after two years of diluted shows and cutesy kiddie comedy, Hill was still very much the target of new wave vehemence and political anger.

In a 1987 interview with *Q* magazine, the 'alternative' comedian Ben Elton famously said: "You have Benny Hill in the late eighties chasing half-naked women around a park, when we know in Britain women can't even walk safe in a park any more … I could say 'fuck' a thousand times on telly and I wouldn't be nearly as offensive as that."

The attack stunned Hill, but his retaliation was weak and unconvincing. He insisted that it was the girls that chased him at the end of every show. This was technically true of course, but they were usually chasing him because he'd mistakenly felt them up or had tried to peer up their dresses.

Benny's public image was further harmed around this time by the British tabloid newspapers. An unhealthy obsession with his wealth and 'miserly' spending habits soon got out of hand. At one point *The Sun* and the *Daily Mirror* were splashing undignified photos of the star over their front pages; he'd been secretly snapped whilst doing his characteristically modest round of shopping. Festooned with plastic bags, dishevelled and distracted, the pictures evoked the pathetic loneliness of Hill, but the copy incited anger over his reputed tight-fistedness. The star lived in a sparsely-furnished two-bedroomed flat and had no car, the headlines blurted, but had drawers stuffed with money and uncashed cheques for hundreds of thousands of pounds. Hill was bemused and bewildered by the vindictiveness of the reporting. Money had never mattered to him. He was simply continuing to live the way he had done for years.

Worse, column inches of the sex-obsessed Sunday tabloids were filling with exposes of Benny's reportedly less-than-savoury behaviour with some of the models and dancers on his shows. Several women sold kiss-and-tell stories, which ranged from detailed descriptions of Benny's mildly eccentric attitudes towards sex to accusations of improper conduct. Hill weathered all this stoically; in private, however, he was unsettled by the changing public perception of him. Although he could never accept it, it was becoming clear that, regardless of international success, in Britain his time was up.

So, in June 1989, as his show was beamed enthusiastically to scores of millions of people in more than 100 countries, Hill found himself walking out into the London sunshine without a job. Of course, a star of his magnitude could have survived a career blow like this, but Hill was not your average global celebrity. If he'd walked into a television studio in almost any city in the world — New York, Los Angeles, Paris, Rome, Tokyo, Moscow, Sydney — it is likely that he could have secured some sort of a deal to continue making his shows. Instead, Hill endured the hurt of being *persona non grata* at Teddington. For twenty years, Thames TV had been the only place he'd wanted to make his series — he didn't like change, his friends were there, and he could walk to work. His friend Dennis Kirkland commented: "Benny was totally and utterly stupefied. These shows were his babies, so when John Howard Davies sacked him it was like losing his family; his whole life; his

Hill gives the "Fred Scuttle" salute.

reason for getting up in the morning."

With the show off the air, Hill's lifeline was severed. And the idea of returning to films was no longer a feasible one. While Hill's film career had seen a
couple of high profile highlights in the late sixties (*Chitty Chitty Bang Bang*
[1968], *The Italian Job* [1969]), the relative failure of *The Waiters* (1971),
his homage to the silent comedy short, had propelled him further into the
safety of television, where he had already proved that he could mimic the
style and simplicity of classical comedy cinema with more success. And, now
in his mid sixties and quite seriously overweight, Hill was not likely to attract
much box office from the all-important youth audience.

His physical decline from this point began to quicken. At a loose end,
friends noticed his already gluttonous appetite for rich living increase markedly. In the months following his sacking, Benny dived into socialising to
deaden the pain. This, inevitably, led to an upsurge of alcohol consumption.
His house cleaner observed him 'drinking sherry straight from the bottle';
Kirkland commented that he 'discovered the joys of pub crawling'; and a
former Hill's Angel watched Hill slowly downing a bottle of vodka as he sat
on his own at a party she'd invited him to.

Although awash with opportunities for appearances on international
television stations, Hill also stopped writing. The almost frantic jotting and
regurgitating of sketch and song ideas on scraps of paper and napkins, which

had been a constant feature of his professional life, ground to a halt. A friend asked him why; he replied: "What's the point?"

Despite the offers Hill was receiving from abroad, his heartbreak would probably not have been eased by relaunching his career in another country. He had been rejected at home, and this left an emotional scar that foreign success could not have healed. It would have been like marrying an unremarkable but willing substitute after being dumped by a true love.

To add insult to injury, even repeats of *The Benny Hill Show* seemed to have become untouchable in Britain. While it continued to play on primetime around the world, Hill saw his show, in the months immediately following his dismissal, more or less vanish from the schedules in the UK. A decade on, it remains unseen in its original format on British terrestrial television.

By the time Hill did to go back to some kind of work, he was visibly in creative and physical decline. Don Taffner had remained loyal to the star, and secured financing for the first of a proposed new series of shows called *Benny Hill's World*, which were aimed more specifically at an American audience. The pilot episode, set in the States, was taped, mostly in the UK, in 1991. The resulting episode was a pale shadow of the comedian's best work, and fared badly even in comparison to the later Thames shows. Mark Lewisohn comments that "the sparkle of the Thames period had disappeared ... drowned in a surfeit of alcohol, over-eating and melancholia." After the production of this first show, Don Taffner met with some delays finding the financing for more episodes of *Benny Hill's World*, and the project stalled. (The resulting pilot was not shown in Britain until two years after Benny's death.)

In his very last TV appearances (in 1991, in the *Omnibus* documentary *Clown Imperial* and chatting on an episode of *Des O' Connor Tonight*), Hill exuded a brittle sadness. Trying to be enthusiastic, there was a trace of pain etched on his face. He looked like a man trying to apologise for himself, but unsure of what he had done wrong. Dutifully, he trotted out some hoary old gags, but with little real spark or conviction.

Hill was now frequently indulging himself in lunchtime brandies and impromptu drinking binges, and clogging up his arteries with chocolate cakes and fried breakfasts. It wasn't going to be long before serious health problems presented themselves. In February 1992, he suffered a heart attack. Although mild, it was a clear warning to the seventeen stone star to alter his lifestyle. On leaving the hospital, specialists told Hill that he could die at any time without opting for urgent bypass surgery. But he was too terrified to go through with it. (As a measure of how famous Benny Hill remained abroad, it is interesting to note that one of his visitors during his stay in hospital was Michael Jackson.)

Ironically, as Hill's health now deteriorated, a number of British TV companies, Thames included, were beginning to express an interest in making some new, revamped Benny Hill shows. Negotiations were ongoing from early 1992. Hill and Kirkland went along with the talks, but it is clear that Hill's heart wasn't in it. However, to tentatively smooth the path to reconciliation, Thames began broadcasting edited versions of some of his later shows.

But the damage was done. Hill spent his final weeks holed up in his flat, trying to catch his breath whilst watching television. Although worth a reputed £7 million, he did not change his modest lifestyle. Hill hadn't been corrupted by his money; he hadn't been comforted by it either. During these last days, his trusted companion Dennis Kirkland helped out with little chores for him. Hill's last trip out, on April 15, 1992, saw him attending a performance of *Me and My Girl* at the Adelphi Theatre, which starred his Hill's Angel protégée, Louise English. English noticed during their backstage chat that Benny's neck 'looked dark, almost blue'.

On April 20, Dennis Kirkland had not been able to get in touch with Benny for a few days. A day earlier, news had broken of Frankie Howerd's death. Hill had been quoted in the press as being very upset about it. But Hill had not actually said this — a journalist had instead phoned Kirkland for Benny's response. That evening, Hill's neighbour called Kirkland and said there was an unpleasant smell coming from the comedian's flat. Kirkland came round, but failed to get a response as he knocked at the door. Climbing a ladder to Hill's second floor balcony, Kirkland looked through the window to see the sixty-eight-year-old star slumped on the sofa, bloated and blue. He had been dead for two days. As usual, the TV was playing. The flat was strewn with papers, videotapes and unwashed plates.

The next night, Thames hurriedly assembled a 'tribute' to Benny Hill, which ran instead of the scheduled repeat of one of his edited-down, half-hour shows. The show featured a stunned Kirkland blankly talking about his late friend in a lifeless studio chat. Just half an hour long, it was a clumsy, dispiriting piece of television. Fitting then, for it to be Thames TV's tribute to the star it ditched so unceremoniously.

[Benny Hill filmography p.146]

Terry-Thomas
Temporarily Embarrassed

On December 8,1988, the UK tabloid newspaper *The Mirror* reported 'exclusively' on 'Comic Terry's Life of Poverty'. Journalist Tony Purnell had found Terry-Thomas, seventy-seven-years-old and suffering the debilitating later stages of Parkinson's Disease, living hand-to-mouth in south-west London. The "veteran comic actor is now so poor," Purnell wrote, "that he has to live off charity in a sparsely-furnished three-roomed flat." Indeed, T-T had been reduced to receiving hand-outs from the Entertainment Artistes' Benevolent Fund and the Parkinson's Disease Society, and was being cared for round

The incorrigible upper class bounder, Terry-Thomas.

the clock by his tirelessly supportive but now struggling wife, Belinda. Their church charity flat was barely heated. Belinda had to make tea by boiling panfuls of water.

The reaction to the piece was profound, with stunned ex-colleagues and a shocked public contacting *The Mirror* over the course of the day to express their concern for the ailing star. *The Mirror* quickly realised that the story 'had legs' and ran another piece, the following morning, that further high-lighted the painfully reduced circumstances of T-T's present condition. "You have to look closely behind the unfamiliar grey beard to recognise the famous, now tragic, face of Terry-Thomas," Tony Purnell wrote on December 9. "The former funnyman, ravaged by years of suffering from the crippling Parkinson's Disease, simply stares blankly into space ... The film world's upper class gent is sadly on his uppers."

The photo accompanying the piece underlined this sensationalist prose, if any underlining was necessary, with a shocking image of an expressionless T-T, lined, gaunt and grey, looking as far removed as possible from the stylish, exuberant dash he cut in the fifties and sixties. Wearing a patchy, stubbly beard and a shapeless woollen cap, he looked like the very embodiment of a man in the gutter.

Even more disturbing — despite the ostensibly good intentions — was Purnell's announcement that *The Mirror* brought a rare twinkle to Terry's eyes when we presented him with a brand-new toaster, an electric kettle and six pairs of warm woollen socks." This was followed with an appeal for monetary support — "Send cheques or postal orders ... to *The Mirror Terry-Thomas Appeal.*" A demeaning fate indeed for one of the sparkiest, most successful and most identifiably British comic film stars of the post-war era.

In the mid sixties, Terry-Thomas was second only to Peter Sellers as Britain's most successful comic export. Although his very best work was just behind him, he was in constant demand as a silly ass Englishman and incorrigible upper class bounder in slinky Hollywood comedies and big-budget international extravaganzas. Usually confined to supporting roles, T-T's name was, nonetheless, frequently third-billed behind contemporary stars of the magnitude of Jack Lemmon and Doris Day. Even in roles that were little more than high profile cameos, T-T, more often than not, stole the show. Highly paid, extremely busy and universally popular, it looked, by the end of the decade, like Terry-Thomas would be facing an extremely comfortable and rewarding future as he settled into late middle age.

Indeed, as the seventies began, T-T kept winning the lucrative contracts — when not in films then in television advertising. As late as 1979, the Ford Motor Company was paying him £5,000 a day for a six-day shoot for a commercial they were making. But by then T-T could barely stop himself from shaking long enough to wrap a thirty-second scene. His Parkinson's Disease, first diagnosed in the early seventies, had by now effectively halted his career.

(Mat 2-A; Still No. N. Y. 11) Comedians Peter Sellers, right, and Terry-Thomas put their heads together with hilarious results in the Boulting Brothers' sensational new comedy, "I'm All Right Jack." Ian Carmichael is also starred in the Columbia release which takes a zany look at labor-management relations.

After the initial diagnosis, T-T had continued to work but less prolifically. This wasn't just an immediate effect of the disease, however. Rather, the kinds of films he had been making in the sixties had rapidly gone out of fashion, or they had become too expensive to contemplate. Instead, he diversified into tongue-in-cheek horror films (*The Abominable Dr. Phibes, Dr. Phibes Rises Again, Vault of Horror*), obscure international co-productions and more TV work, notably in commercials of the kind mentioned above. His last leading 'Terry-Thomas' role for the big screen was in 1975's *Spanish Fly*, a lame and rather grubby Menorca-set sex farce, which nonetheless gave him the opportunity to lock horns with the equally caddish Leslie Phillips. Soon after, his Parkinson's Disease began to show itself more conspicuously, and was clearly in evidence in the following year's Marty Feldman vehicle *The Last Remake of Beau Geste* (1976).

Cruel rumours began to spread, as is so often the case in showbiz, that T-T's increasingly visible shakes owed more to the DTs than to illness. Terry countered this in 1977 by becoming a celebrity spokesman for the Parkinson's Disease Society. By this time, however, he could no longer commit himself to film roles or television series. He made cameo appearances in just two more films, the woeful *Hound of the Baskervilles* (1977) and another obscure Europudding, *Febbre a 40/Happy Birthday Harry* (1980), before bowing out of film acting completely.

T-T had lived on the island of Ibiza for many years and was now resigned to coping with his illness at least with the help of the Spanish sun. But as comfortably off as he was as the eighties began, very soon his medical bills began to consume his fortune. In 1983, T-T and his wife moved into a villa in Majorca, which his ex-wife had left to him after her death. This enabled him to put their Ibiza home on the market for £250,000.

During this time, Terry decided to collaborate with a journalist friend, Terry Baum, on writing his memoirs before it was too late. But the period in which the majority of the book was written (1983–84) saw the most serious decline in T-T's condition and standard of living. Baum noted that where, in Ibiza, T-T and his wife had five large kitchens, in Majorca they now had one tiny one. And where they had once been used to servants, Belinda now "had to dress and wash Terry every morning, assist him whenever he went to the lavatory, bath him, administer enemas, give him all his pills at the right time, massage him and change his slippers at two-hourly intervals ..." On top of this, she found herself having to do "the usual household chores, shopping and answering their correspondence".

At the beginning of the project, T-T could on occasion be animated enough to recount a good story and give his ghost writer plenty of material, even if the writer did have to draw it out of him. But often his memory for names and films and punch lines was harmed by the disease, and as the book neared its first draft completion, "it became more and more difficult for him to recall anecdotes and certainly not funny ones." Indeed, on some days, the writer could not make any progress as T-T was "either too unwell to begin a conversation, or having begun, would suddenly lapse into silence and stare aimlessly at the ground."

T-T himself was forced to drop his carefully constructed guard and confess to the tormenting frustration of Parkinson's Disease during the writing of

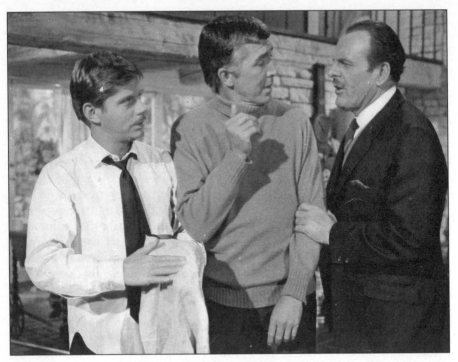

T-T in Hollywood. ***Where Were You When the Lights Went Out***

the book. "Largely because of being dominated by the disease," he wrote, "I have become more and more of a recluse. Owing to the sense of confusion it causes, I find it very difficult to behave naturally without shaking and I'm not keen to be seen like this in public, a shadow of my former self." He also pointed to the financial pain the illness was causing: "I try not to dwell on the fact that my being struck by the disease prevented me from amassing another little fortune. Now that we are going through a long, protracted period of inflation, just like everyone else I can see my savings dwindling rapidly ..."

Publishing the memoirs may have kept the wolf from the door for a little while longer, but T-T's perfectionism prevented him from authorising its publication. The book wasn't, in his opinion, funny enough, and he struggled to revise the manuscript whenever he felt up to it. But even on good days, he could only concentrate for a number of minutes, and when he had the energy to jot something in the margin, it was invariably just a minor alteration instead of a humorous addition. By 1985, it was clear to Baum that T-T would never finish his mooted 'revisions'. Weeks, months and then years passed without any progress on the original manuscript. T-T had high standards to maintain, and justified his caution on one occasion by telling Baum that he "wanted to be remembered as a comedian". "That was the last time I ever heard him speak," Baum said. "On my subsequent visits to Bonanova he had given up talking. He would be sitting in a chair staring blankly into space... The manuscript would always be near by, but not often

T-T with Vincent Price. **The Abominable Dr Phibes**

open... He had become thin, hollow-eyed and shrunken."

Terry and his increasingly weary wife were forced to sell the Majorcan place and move back to England. That was when *The Mirror* came knocking.

Two days after *The Mirror* broke the first story of Terry's hardship, it proudly reported that his 'stunned friends' had rallied to his aid. Cash donations had begun to come in, and showbiz colleagues expressed their dismay at how such a great man could end up in such circumstances. Bob Monkhouse, who donated £1,000 to Terry's appeal, had no idea the star was in such a position. "I thought he was still comfortably off and still living in the Spanish sunshine," he said.

Early in 1989, Richard Hope-Hawkins and the actor Thorley Walters visited T-T and reported that "the face that we saw was not that of a man that we knew and loved but that of a man wracked with pain ..." They also elaborated on the pitiful state of his living arrangements: "There is no running water and the only form of heating is provided by a small gas fire." They noted that Terry's family's lives "are taken up with continuous rounds of washing and the arduous task of spoon-feeding him at least three times a day."

Fuelled into action, Hope-Hawkins got together with the former *Carry On* actor Jack Douglas to plan a benefit concert for the star. Douglas hastily recruited a plethora of largely B-list actors and comedians (Roy Castle, Barbara Windsor, Janet Brown), TV personalities (sports presenter Frank Bough!), musicians and dancers (the Palladium Girls, the Richard Holmes Orchestra) and put together The Terry-Thomas Benefit concert, which graced the stage of the Theatre Royal Drury Lane on April 9, 1989. The evening raised £75,000, due in no small part to the surprise participation of British comedy fan Phil Collins, who was then a pretty hot property. It was a well-intended, heartfelt entertainment — pretty ropey stuff, but that's how Brits always liked their variety shows. But if the live entertainment was creaky, then at least the pre-recorded tributes reminded the audience of T-T's international importance — they were given by the likes of Julie Andrews, Jack Lemmon, Dudley Moore and Mickey Rooney.

On the proceeds of the night, T-T was moved to a modestly comfortable nursing home in Godalming, Surrey. "His face showed no emotion at all but I shall never forget Terry's eyes," Jack Douglas commented. "They shone when he saw the nursing home. Here was this man saying "Thank you" with his eyes." T-T, now seventy-eight, was to live in this relative comfort only for another four months, however. Sadly, his devoted wife Belinda could not be at his bedside during his final hours. The pressure of the last few months had been too much for her and when T-T died, from chest complications on January 8, 1990, she was in a clinic recovering from a nervous breakdown.

A few months later, Terry Baum published T-T's memoirs, *Terry-Thomas Tells Tales*, which, although never achieving "perfectionist Terry's criterion", stood as his 'final performance' and served as a useful reminder of one of Britain's greatest comedy characters.

[*Terry-Thomas filmography p.147*]

Barry Evans
Misadventures of a
Taxi Driver

By the mid 1990s, millions of Brits knew of a Barry Evans. As played by Shaun Williamson, he was a fictional character in BBC TV's *EastEnders*. Fat, befuddled and ever optimistic, Barry Evans provided welcome comic relief in a soap that continues to be drenched in misery and antagonism.

At the same time, however, a real Barry Evans — a former actor, an ex-celebrity — could not have been much further removed from this nominal counterpart. He too had once brought smiles to the nation's faces, as a jovial, fresh-faced and gifted comic performer. But now he was broke, drunk,

Barry Evans

depressed and reduced to a menial job. And in February 1997, he was found dead in mysterious circumstances.

The wide-eyed, brown-haired Evans was one of the most amiable comedy stars of the seventies. On television he was the handsome and vulnerable Michael Upton in the schedule-swamping *Doctor* sitcoms. Later, he was the well-meaning teacher in the broadly popular comedy, *Mind Your Language*. For a while, no British weekend was complete without Evans beaming into the living room. On the big screen, he had less success, but for a time he ranked somewhere near Robin Askwith as the kind of cheeky lothario that people forked out money to see in a couple of ropey Britcom features.

The later sex comedies may have been abysmal, but Evans' chirpy perform-ance as the hapless sixth former Jamie MacGregor in his first screen outing — the risqué (for its time) *Here We Go Round the Mulberry Bush* (1967) — was one of the most charming screen debuts of its day. Like *Gregory's Girl* a decade later, *Mulberry Bush* was a landmark sex comedy that centred on an awkward, naïve and comically frustrated adolescent. And where *Grego-*

*Evans and **Mind Your Language** on the cover of children's TV comic **Look-In***
(cover dated October 14 and December 9, 1978).

ry's Girl was a breath of fresh air that helped finally to blow away the tired embers of the brainless British sex comedy, *Mulberry Bush* was the breeze of permissiveness that had effectively started it. In retrospect, the smutty sex comedy seems to have taken Evans down with it.

In 1969, though, the world, or at least Britain, was Evans' oyster. At twenty-five, he moved immediately into dependable TV familiarity in two successive *Doctor* series (*Doctor in the House* and *Doctor at Large*), cramming in sixty episodes in two years. Likeable, innocent and intrigued by — yet somehow fearful of — the opposite sex, Evans was the kind of boy a modern girl could confidently present to her conservative parents before submitting to him in the back of his Vauxhall Viva

Good as he was at these kinds of roles, Evans also hankered for a more serious profile. He quit the *Doctor* series and drastically changed direction, turning up as Susan George's co-star in Peter Walker's lurid pulp thriller, *Die Screaming Marianne* (1972). But such hysterical tack did little to further his straight acting career. Maybe there were signs that it was going to be Walker's breakthrough film; it wasn't. Nevertheless, Evans did not return to his comfortable sitcom persona for another five years, and the *Doctor* series carried on without him.

In his absence from the small screen, Evans concentrated on the theatre, and for a while directed plays at Theatr Clwyd in Mold, although this work was interspersed with lengthy periods on the dole. In 1975 he signed up for the first of Stanley Long's imitative *Adventures* film series, but *Adventures of a Taxi Driver* was dire even in comparison to the *Confessions* movies, and it has to be said that Evans' saucy boyishness was already beginning to look weary by this time. Rather than being funny, the star appears a bit disturbed by his own seediness in the film, especially running around naked from the waist down, which just didn't seem *right* somehow. Nevertheless, *Adventures* was a domestic moneymaker (and was still doing the business as an early video hit five years later), providing one of the big screen roles that Evans, whether he liked it or not, became most closely associated with.

Evans didn't return for the second *Adventures* film (Christopher Neil, a few years away from being Sheena Easton's music producer, took over). This might have looked like good sense had he not stooped even lower for the dismal *Under the Doctor* (1976), another groaning example of what passed for soft porn comedy in Britain in the seventies.

Clearly, the film career was not going to plan, so a near-desperate Evans approached London Weekend Television for more TV work. LWT offered him the role of Jeremy Brown, an English teacher struggling to communicate with a class of enthusiastic but confused immigrants. The show was *Mind Your Language*.

Immensely popular (at the time), *Mind Your Language* (1977–79) restored Evans to the public's affection by demanding of him the kind of characterisation he'd tried so hard to get away from — the boyish, hapless hero. Still, he brought his customary comic warmth and enthusiasm to the role. He was at least sympathetic and endearing — a confrontational actor might have

exacerbated the racist implications of the show. Even so, the passage of time has not been kind to *Mind Your Language*. In the politically correct 1980s, the series quickly became an embarrassment. Despite reaching audiences of eighteen million at its peak, it was buried in the archives (probably next to *Love Thy Neighbour*) and no episode has been re-run on British terrestrial TV for twenty years. (Quite bizarrely, however, Albert Moses, who played a student in the series, turned producer in 1986 and independently funded thirteen more episodes of *Mind Your Language*, starring Evans and most of the original cast. But such was the socio-politi-

Diana Dors plays Barry Evans' mother in
Adventures of a Taxi Driver.

cal and cultural climate by then that it was pushed aside; in the UK the full series was shown in the north west region only — and at 2pm on Saturdays, a slot reserved almost exclusively for low profile sporting events.)

So, as the eighties progressed, Evans sank into inactivity and, as a result, obscurity. He continued to work sporadically on provincial theatre tours, but serious screen work eluded him. Maybe he had become a casualty of the changing times, but others like him (and some less talented) seemed to survive that transition from carefree to PC, at least for a while — Richard O' Sullivan, Robin Askwith, George Layton, for instance.

In 1993, despondent with show business, Evans quit London and went to live, in a 'rundown bungalow', in Claybrooke Magna, Leicestershire. Ironically, given his most famous film role, he was forced to make a living as a taxi driver. Things got worse from there. He began to drink heavily. Towards the end of his life, it was said, he was putting away a bottle of whisky every two days. He'd failed as an actor, and this was not the kind of behaviour that was going to guarantee success in the cab-driving business either. The mood swings and depression worsened. On good days he showed videos of his old shows and films to friends and talked about getting back into acting, but he never made any serious effort to do so.

In February 1997, Evans contacted the police to report that his car had been stolen. When the police went to his house to inform him that they had recovered it, they found Evans dead, lying face down, fully clothed, on the sofa. He was fifty-two.

Just hours later, police arrested and held two young men and a girl, who had been caught in Evans' stolen car before he was found dead. The picture that was forming was one of an attempted robbery that had ended in homicide. Obituaries and news pieces began to report that Evans had died from a blow to the head. On April 25, one of the youths, an eighteen-year old man, was charged with attempted murder.

In January 1998, however, the case against the teenager was dropped. The Crown Prosecution Service admitted that there was 'no real prospect' of a conviction against him. He had always denied the charge, and no physical evidence seemed to corroborate the 'blow to the head' story. It was now suggested that Evans had poisoned himself with drink and drugs.

In October 1998, the coroner for Leicester and South Leicestershire recorded an open verdict on Evans' death. Evidently, the actor had been found with four and a half times the legal drink limit in his blood, but the coroner could not conclude that Evans had deliberately drunk himself to death.

Some of the details that did emerge around the time of the coroner's report do encourage the notion that Evans had wanted to kill himself. He had apparently made a will just days before his death. And a spilled bottle of aspirins (which, bizarrely, was priced 'before decimalisation') was found next to his body, although he hadn't taken any. This led the coroner, Martin Symington, to ask: "Was he perhaps contemplating taking the tablets and the alcohol together, but passed out before he could use the tablets?" That might be feasible, but it also seems a bit farcical — wanting to kill yourself and then dying by accident before you get around to it. It's the stuff of black comedy.

But for every conventional attempted suicide or accidental death angle, there were as many unusual circumstances surrounding Evans' demise. His credit cards were missing and, as already mentioned, his car had been stolen. Strangest of all, he apparently rang a friend at five in the morning and left a message asking to be called back. The friend tried to return the call but couldn't get through. Evidently, Evans' telephone line was now not working. The plot thickens. Since then, however, no new evidence has come to light that points to murder, whether intentional or not.

The mystery of Evans' death may one day be more satisfactorily explained. But the story of the decline and fall of a good comic actor, and his inability to shake free of the boyishly confused roles, even in middle age, will always grate on his fans and friends. His performance in *Adventures of a Taxi Driver* — frequently rebroadcast on Channel 5 in Britain — as the chirpy, cocksure cabbie, extolling the amorous virtues of his profession, now has an unsettlingly tragic irony to it. A sad epitaph was provided by one of Evans' Claybrooke Magna neighbours at the time of his death: "When he first came to this area, everyone knew him as Barry the actor, but over the years he just became Barry the taxi driver."

The year before his death, a newspaper tracked Evans down and found him 'helping out' at a friend's hotel in Leicester. He talked a little about going back to acting. In another twist of irony, given that his fictional namesake was now on the box three times a week, he admitted: "What I want is a long run in *EastEnders*."

[*Barry Evans filmography p.148*]

Peter Cook
A Life in Pieces

When Peter Cook died at the beginning of 1995, no obituary failed to address the question of whether or not his potential had ever been properly fulfilled, or whether the last twenty years of his life had been wasted. And of course, no obituary could avoid discussing what effect Dudley Moore's astounding (if short-lived) solo Hollywood success might have had on him during this final, frequently trouble period of his life. What is clear is that the loss of Moore — as a comedy sounding board, a stooge, an improvisation partner and a professional whipping boy — left Cook, for all his proven ability, foundering professionally, and coincided with a steep decline in his personal life.

But the rot was starting to set into Cook's life long before Dudley broke away and was launched into the big time with '*10*'(1979). As early as 1970, Cook was sampling his first taste of failure and disillusionment, and this was particularly hard to bear after a decade of seemingly unstoppable success.

Cook had, up to that point, scaled dazzling heights with everything he had put his mind to. By 1962, at the age of twenty-five, he had achieved success on the West End and on Broadway with the ground-breaking *Beyond the Fringe*, established 'The Establishment' — Britain's first satirical comedy club — and assumed ownership of the subversive magazine *Private Eye*. And from the beginning of his career, Cook was seen as the first among equals. Few other comic performers and writers have been so heralded by their peers; few others were so widely labelled 'genius' not just for their achievements but also for their sparklingly witty company. And, despite the later decline, no-one got away with as much as Cook did, who, right up to the end of his life, when any kind of real conventional success eluded him, continued to be worshipped as a mentor by each new generation of comedians.

In 1965 Cook properly cemented his partnership with fellow Fringer Dudley Moore and began two successful BBC series of *Not Only... But Also*, a milestone of British television comedy that helped pave the way for *Monty Python* and a host of semi-surreal and 'subversive' imitators. This, in turn, led to a film deal with Twentieth Century Fox, the first fruit of which was the occasionally hilarious if somewhat ham-fisted *Bedazzled* (1967).

Although not altogether successful, *Bedazzled* showed great promise. By the late sixties, then, Cook and Moore had only film left to conquer. And although they were offered a steady stream of work in films, like *Monte Carlo or Bust* (1969) and *The Bed Sitting Room* (1969), Cook was already getting bored. His true ambition was to crack this medium alone. Fearful of repeating himself, he wanted to ditch Dudley and become a film star in his own right, and given his track record, there seemed no reason why he shouldn't succeed.

*Peter Cook
in a publicity
shot taken
whilst filming
Bedazzled.*

In 1970, the project Cook was resting all his faith in was *The Rise and Rise of Michael Rimmer*, a political satire financed by David Frost, in which Cook played the lead. But this project was a crushing failure, and for the first time it exposed one of Cook's chronic weaknesses: he couldn't act. Of course, he had performed admirably in revue and television sketches, but there is a world of difference between a three-minute skit with a punchline (or without one, as the case may be) and carrying the weight of a film. In his earlier films, particularly *Bedazzled*, Cook had had the more sympathetic Moore to play off, but even here he was curiously stilted, somewhat ill-at-ease. *Michael Rimmer*, however, proved beyond doubt that he was flawed as an actor, and would never make it as a leading man.

This failure was the first real knock-back Cook had felt since his career began, and for the first time he found himself returning to past glories. He embarked on a third BBC series of *Not Only... But Also* with Dudley, but despite its success he remained somewhat despondent. Still keen to broaden his horizons alone, he tried in 1971 to establish himself as a chat show host.

Where Do I Sit?, however, was a disaster of the first order, although Cook's character Arthur Streeb-Greebling might disagree, preferring to call it 'a catastrophe'. Transmitted live, it was a shambolic travesty of the talk show genre. Cook proved to be a desperately bad host, unable to interview guests properly and lapsing into awkward silences and inappropriate tirades as the programmes invariably slipped completely out of his control. Its cancellation after just three episodes left him with two keenly-felt professional humiliations in less than twelve months. Coupled with the acrimonious split from his wife Wendy that was simultaneously dogging his life, it wasn't long before Cook was over-indulging in drink and drugs to mask the pain.

Once again, he returned to the Pete and Dud partnership, and accepted an offer to tour Australia with a new two-man show called *Behind the Fridge*. The show was extremely well-received, but the seeds of disruption had been sown, and there was no getting away from the fact that the duo were falling back on their laurels when the energy to create new material deserted them. In his perceptive biography of Cook, Harry Thompson writes: "by the time they left for Australia in September 1971, Peter had completed the last truly substantial piece of work he would ever write."

Despite being temporarily revitalised by the tour's warm reception Down Under, Peter, with his marital problems and professional *ennui* escalating, soon fell further into the grip of alcohol. One evening he had to be fished, fully clothed, from a swimming pool before a performance. On another night, Michael Parkinson, in the audience, remembers seeing Dudley 'literally holding Peter up' throughout the show. Remarkably, the Australian audience either didn't notice, or turned a blind eye to such chaos — and *Behind the Fridge* continued its successful run.

When the show opened in London at the end of 1972, Cook was so drunk beforehand that he fell unconscious and had to be force fed black coffee before being literally pushed onto the stage by its director. Nevertheless, *Behind the Fridge* carried on, to generally favourable reviews and enthusiastic box office, for another year, whereupon its two stars were lured to take it to the US for a handsome remuneration.

Retitled *Good Evening*, the revue was rapturously received in US, and its ongoing success masked the stars' crumbling relationship, as well as Peter's complete reliance on drink and drugs. Yet Peter was now on auto-pilot, cruising through material that was by now years old. And the show's success wasn't bringing him personal happiness.

But it was Dudley who, after finding it harder and harder to work with the increasingly alcoholic Cook, effectively ended their ten-year partnership when *Good Evening* finished its run in LA in August 1975. And by now it was Dudley who was more keen to succeed alone. He set up home in Hollywood (with his new wife Tuesday Weld) and began to make himself available for film work. Peter, by contrast, had no idea what to do next.

The Cook/Moore partnership would not die out easily, however. By the time of this 'split', the word-of-mouth success of several audio sketches they had casually recorded for their own amusement in 1973 was growing rapidly. As foul-mouthed toilet cleaners Derek and Clive, Cook and Moore had

Dudley Moore and Peter Cook. **Bedazzled**

waxed lyrical in X-rated head-to-heads that were peppered with inventive profanities and risqué songs. Such was the success of this bootleg tape that, in 1976, Island Records released it, with some extra material, as *Derek and Clive (Live)*.

Somewhat unexpectedly, the recording was a hit on both sides of the Atlantic, and its success led to another film deal. The partnership was thus temporarily rekindled, albeit with some reluctance from Dudley, who, although desperate to relaunch his film career, was not over-keen on re-teaming with Cook.

In any event, the resulting film project, *The Hound of the Baskervilles* (1977) was a monumental misfire. Directed by, of all people, Paul Morrissey of Andy Warhol's Factory fame, *Hound* deliberately attempted to recreate the grotesquely comic essence of the better *Carry On* films, but instead descended into a juvenile circus of smutty puns, overblown acting and misjudged timing. By many accounts, the script for the film, largely written by Cook, had been funny. What turned up on the screen, however, was nothing more than a witless farrago. Cook's comedy was not compatible with *Carry On*; indeed, it could barely have been more different. Still, the American director Morrissey can not be expected to shoulder all the blame — Moore and Cook knew their own style, yet they act throughout the film as if they are deliberately trying to wreck it.

Regardless of intention, *The Hound of the Baskervilles* was so bad that its distributors (Hemdale) sat on it for the best part of eighteen months before quietly releasing it, whereupon it was annihilated by the critics and ignored by the public.

Cook shrugged off the attacks, but was privately mortified by them. Now contracted to two more Derek and Clive albums, Dudley and Peter recorded *Come Again* in one day at the end of 1977 before Dudley went back to Hollywood. By the time he returned for the final album, *Ad Nauseam*, the following year, Dudley had made the most of a funny cameo in the Goldie Hawn/Chevy Chase comedy *Foul Play* (1978) and was starting to make a splash in LA. Thus the dynamic between the performers was changing.

Tellingly, *Ad Nauseam*, while managing to be even more obscene than the first two Derek and Clive records (the highlights included a routine about wanking over a TV broadcast of the pope's funeral, and the ditty 'I'm a Nigger and I Fucked a White Chick') also clearly showed a double act that was descending into hostility and abuse — most of it from Peter. After its recording, Dudley vowed not to work with Cook again. He had been offered his first leading role in Hollywood, helping out Blake Edwards, whose production '10' had been thrown into crisis when George Segal had walked off the set.

With such troubled beginnings, no-one quite expected that '10' would go through the roof, but it did. Something about its undemanding, vulgar comedy, trendy self-analysis and tentative promiscuity caught the mood of the nation, as Hollywood straddled the bridge of the sordid yet progressive seventies and the puritanical, mindless eighties. The film cleaned up at the box office. By the end of 1979, Dudley was an A-list Hollywood star.

Cook's public attitude to Dudley's newfound stardom wavered from the sarcastically vicious to the tentatively proud. (He famously said that he would

have been eager to be loved by millions too, if he'd been a club-footed dwarf like Dudley.) But it was clear that Peter was keen to emulate his former partner's Stateside success. In 1981, he accepted a leading role in a new US sitcom, *The Two of Us*, which saw him cast as a quintessentially English butler. The show started promisingly, but could not sustain its appeal over the required twenty-four episode run. In March 1982, as Dudley was coasting on another massive Hollywood hit (*Arthur*), *The Two of Us* was cancelled.

When they had been working together, Cook and Moore had each other to support (or blame) when projects didn't turn out the way they would have liked. But now, as Harry Thompson comments, "for the first time, Peter was shouldering the burden of failure entirely alone."

Returning to the UK, Peter's marriage to his second wife, Judy, finally broke down. Although they had been soul mates from the beginning, with Judy tolerating Peter's frequent infidelity out of sheer adoration for his charm and lovability, Peter's increasing depressive, alcoholic rages had destroyed the relationship. Judy had to put a restraining order on her husband, even though they had continued to share the same house. Now, she finally made the break, and Peter was left to face the eighties alone — both personally and professionally.

Dudley continued to play the Hollywood success story, even though the reception to his films was starting to cool, but Peter fell into a destructive routine of loafing and drinking, working only sporadically. He was still capable of great comic invention when the mood took him, but this was rarely in front of a camera or even at a professional engagement. Instead, he whiled away the boredom by phoning into his local radio station, pretending to be a Norwegian fisherman. In the event, he surreptitiously provided a couple of hours of quality comic entertainment (free of charge) for LBC's *Clive Bull Show*. But these ostensibly anonymous contributions were never in danger of reviving his career — Clive Bull's show went out from one until four in the morning.

During this time, Peter finally let go of his looks, which saw his white hair become unwashed and unkempt, his fashion sense take on a surreal blend of eccentricity and functionality, and his weight balloon. When he did appear, in the mid eighties, on chat shows and the like, he cut a rather alarming figure, his voice raspy and throaty from years of heavy smoking. His drinking was no longer pleasurable, it was a daily necessity.

Peter had continued to put in the odd undemanding film appearance, easy and infrequent work that kept the bills paid, but the resulting movies were lacklustre fodder: *Supergirl* (1984), *Whoops Apocalypse* (1986), *Without a Clue* (1988). More demeaningly, he also spent a period as Joan Rivers' 'straight man', on her BBC chat show *Can We Talk?* (1986). This surely was his lowest professional point: as Joan chatted with the star guests, Peter sat on the end of the sofa, supposedly bringing a comic balance to the proceedings. More often than not, however, he just looked awkward and barely opened his mouth.

By 1989, Peter was virtually unemployable. Staving off the boredom with alcohol and cocaine or ecstasy, he spent his days like a listless hobo addict, drinking himself to oblivion because it was better than being sober. But there was some good fortune on the horizon. He finally married his casual girlfriend, Lin Chong, and she started to bring some order to his affairs, as well as boost his confidence with much needed love and companionship.

Lin urged Peter to re-enter the world of 'showbiz', and engineered an upturn in his social life that saw him fraternising with new comedians like Harry Enfield, as well as renewing his friendships with old colleagues like John Cleese. More importantly, Lin also smoothed the path for a more reconciliatory relationship with Dudley Moore; feelings between the two men had cooled sharply during the eighties.

Peter began working a little again, and appeared to be getting his act together, albeit slowly. His inspired turn on the chat show *Clive Anderson Talks Back* in 1993 (in which he appeared in three fictional guises) saw him slimmed down and handsome again, and was something of an uplifting event for his fans. He was still drinking heavily — against doctor's orders — but now it was on a more social (i.e. networking) scale than it had been at its worst. Even so, the booze had clearly dampened his talent — much of his TV work in the early nineties was blighted by the spectre of *ennui* and overindulgence. The *Clive Anderson* appearance, then, looked like the beginning of a new and happier chapter.

But less than a year later, Peter was spiralling downwards again: out of shape and desperately unhappy. The catalyst for this downturn was the death of his mother, which affected him so badly it seemed beyond reason. With characteristically weak self-discipline, he returned to the bottle with a vengeance, shocking his friends with the severity of his latest decline. One of his last projects, the comedy golfing video *Peter Cook Talks Balls*, was a dispiriting piece of work. Peter was clearly light years away from his best mental and physical form.

In December 1994, the years of indulgence began to catch up with Peter Cook's health, and he was admitted to hospital for treatment on his liver. Several days later, he collapsed at his London home and was taken to the Royal Free Hospital, where he fell into a coma after throwing up blood. He remained in a coma until his death six days later, on January 9, 1995, aged fifty-seven. The cause of death was given as gastro-intestinal haemorrhage.

Humphrey Carpenter concludes his book on the British satire boom of the sixties, *That Was Satire That Was*, by quoting Nicholas Luard's assessment of the tragedy of Peter Cook: "Peter didn't go into a decline. He was simply bored. He found too much absurdity, too much pretension, too much vanity, and in the end he couldn't really be bothered." This seems to be more fitting than a lament over a loss of talent, or of a career destroyed by misfortune and bad timing. But in view of what he had achieved as a young man, Peter Cook did lose something of his passion, and something of his commitment to seeing things through. And with that he lost something of himself, he lost what had put him into his exalted position in the first place.

Right up to the end of his life, Cook had many opportunities but, in truth, wasted them. When he wanted to develop an idea for television, BBC producers and script editors, most of whom revered him, were more than happy to try and accommodate him. But even then, the few projects that did see the light of day — the TV show *A Life in Pieces* and the radio series *Why Bother?* — were hampered by an onset of lethargy somewhere along the way.

Throughout the late eighties and nineties, the performances he gave on talk shows and panel games were almost without exception sluggish and lacklustre, and constantly failed to live up to the weight of expectation. His league of fans were yearning for him to be funny and brilliant, but such instances were rare and mercurially brief. On *Have I Got News For You*, a direct descendant of the satirical boom Cook had been a part of, he paled into the background as regular panellists Paul Merton and (Cook protégé) Ian Hislop held court. On *Whose Line Is It Anyway?*, the improvisatory comedy show, he was quite useless, and looked utterly disinterested in embracing the spirit of the game, despite being well-known for stream-of-conscious improvisations that could spiral into comic hysteria. On the spleen-venting chat show *Room 101*, he was only mildly amusing in a format that he could and should have excelled in. Even his much-heralded appearance on *Clive Anderson Talks Back* failed to evoke the hilarity of the best of Pete and Dud or even Derek and Clive. Although he had been closer here to retrieving some of the old Peter Cook, he found it all too easy to give up when the acclaim had died down.

Still, if Peter Cook was a fallen star in reality, in the (culturally powerful) eyes of those who adored him, he was forgiven all failings. In the Oxbridge corridors of BBC light entertainment and the pseudo-subversive halls of alternative comedy, he barely lost an ounce of credibility, even though he was clearly losing everything else: his passion, his drive, his energy, his looks, his health.

Cook's comic partner, on the other hand, was never afforded quite the same amount of reverence. But, as a mainstream entertainer, Dudley Moore fell from even greater heights, and ultimately, cut a more tragic figure.

[Peter Cook filmography p.149]

Dudley Moore

On the Rocks

To gauge the extent of Dudley Moore's decline in terms of his personal life and his film career, one only has to compare Oscar Night 1982 with Oscar Night 1994. In 1982, Moore was basking in the success of *Arthur* (1981), which had grossed more than $100 million, and had landed him a Best Actor nomination as reward. Somewhat incongruously, the diminutive lad from

Dudley Moore playing piano with the Birmingham
Symphony Orchestra, October 3, 1969.

Dagenham was competing with Henry Fonda, Burt Lancaster, Warren Beatty and Paul Newman for the statuette. He didn't win it, of course, but that was not the point. The point was he'd arrived.

To underline that fact, Moore and Liza Minnelli did some spiel onstage during the Academy Award ceremony, surely the most high profile live gig any performer will experience. And Dudley suddenly had film offers coming out of his ears. Already in the can or being lined up were *Six Weeks*, *Lovesick*, *Romantic Comedy* and *Unfaithfully Yours*. A few months earlier, Blake Edwards had asked him to take over the role of Inspector Clouseau in a new series of *Pink Panther* movies, following Peter Sellers' death. Moore had wisely turned that offer down. But that he was offered it at all pointed to the fact that he was now a genuine box office draw — the most successful English actor currently in Hollywood.

Oscar Night 1994 was a different kettle of fish. Moore hadn't made a film in three years, and he hadn't had a hit in at least ten. He was busy with music, as ever, but the acting work had dried up. Consequently, he wasn't on the guest list for the Dorothy Chandler Pavillion that night. But he did find himself thrust into the spotlight again — late in the evening he was arrested on suspicion of 'co-habitational abuse'.

Suddenly, millions of people who'd tuned into the Oscars saw Dudley

Moore's LAPD mug shot as it was beamed to TV news channels around the globe. His girlfriend, Nicole Rothschild, had called the police and claimed that the star had tried to choke her as they watched the ceremony on television. Maybe the frustration of his faltering career had got to him. Maybe the volatile Rothschild had wound cuddly Dudley up to snapping point. It transpired that Moore had also called the police, alleging that his wife had assaulted *him* — not unfeasible given her physical superiority and allegedly aggressive nature. Anyway, it was all sorted out, with the couple making open declarations of forgiveness and everlasting love in the newspapers in the days ahead. But it was an embarrassing episode for Moore, and one that did his declining image no favours.

Bizarrely, two weeks later, the couple got married. One wedding guest remembers Dudley looking 'bewildered' at the ceremony. With hindsight, this observation seems particularly portentous. Later, the photographers and assembled press screamed with laughter as Dudley kept losing his balance and falling into the sand as he and Nicole posed for pictures on the beach. But Dudley didn't seem to be laughing.

Although in Britain Moore had been a star since the early sixties, in the US, where he had relocated in the mid seventies, he had been relatively unknown at first. His legendary partnership with Peter Cook — on TV, in revue, on record and in film — had passed generally unnoticed in mainstream US culture. Moore was keen to break into Hollywood films, but it had proved difficult. Eventually, he relied on a couple of good breaks and being in the right place at the right time. Chevy Chase, a fan, got him a cameo in *Foul Play* (1978), in which Moore acquitted himself more than admirably. Then, George Segal walked off the set of *'10'* (1979) leaving the filming schedule in chaos. Director Blake Edwards remembered the affable, entertaining Moore from the group therapy sessions they both attended, and quickly offered him Segal's part. The rest is history — *'10'* was an astronomical success and Moore got his first taste of superstardom. Two years later, *Arthur* further consolidated this. Although not specifically written for Moore, it soon became quite unthinkable to imagine anyone else in the role of the playful, drunken millionaire.

But the story post-*Arthur*, as far as movies were concerned, was a catalogue of failure. For whatever reason — bad judgement on Moore's part, unfair critical reaction, or just because they were unlucky films — none of his further work came anywhere near to being a similar-sized hit. *Best Defense* (1984) was appalling. *Santa Claus* (1985) desperate. *Like Father, Like Son* (1987) completely inconsequential. *Arthur 2* (1988) wasn't all that bad, but was nonetheless savagely attacked. *Crazy People* (1990) perhaps the best of this later bunch, still sank without trace. The unfeasibility of Moore the sex symbol and A-list movie star took hold in the nation's psyche as quickly as his 'overnight' success. By the beginning of the nineties, Dudley Moore was no longer sought for leading Hollywood roles.

Even during his periods of great success, however, Moore had never achieved happiness. His childhood had been so traumatic — underprivileged, unloved, lonely, ashamed of his size and disability — that Moore had

Dudley Moore, Sir John Gielgud and Liza Minnelli. **Arthur**

developed a kind of anhedonia. As with so many stars who began life in deeply unhappy or extremely dysfunctional circumstances, success, beautiful wives, fame and fortune could not close up the raw wound that their formative years had left.

When Dudley was born, club-footed, with a withered left leg shorter than his right, his mother was appalled and held him above her head shouting, "This isn't my baby." When he was a small child, Dudley's mother openly confessed to him that she had wanted to kill him at birth, rather than have him (and her) suffer the pain and shame of the deformity. Such blunt declarations of maternal disappointment left young Dudley feeling that his misshapen leg was a physical manifestation of his inadequacy as a human being. He once claimed that he didn't receive his first hug until he was seven, and then it was from a hospital nurse.

Young Dudley had to endure weeks and weeks during the war alone in hospital, his family unable to visit him regularly, undergoing operation after painful operation. If that wasn't damaging enough, he was shorter than everyone else his age — by the time he was 5'2" he'd reached his full height. Needless to say, he was routinely bullied and humiliated at school.

The one thing Dudley did have though was a fierce intelligence and an uncanny ability with music. That was his ticket out of Dagenham and, ultimately, to Oxford University, Fringe review, television fame and beautiful women. But all that could not take away the damage of those early years, and all the women in the world could not give him the attention that he'd wanted from his mother. He was mixed up, and prone to prolonged bouts of depression and introspection. These were the traits that were to overwhelm him when things were not going so well in his career.

The tabloid circus that had accompanied Moore's domestic disputes in 1994 had also revealed the increasingly chaotic nature of the star's home life. Moore had bought a house for Nicole close to himself, in which Nicole's ex-husband, a drug addict with full-blown AIDS, also resided. The ex-husband reportedly made himself useful about the place, attending to domestic chores and keeping Moore company. But he was also prone to stealing from the star and, on more than one occasion, tried to sell salacious details of Moore's private life to the tabloid newspapers to get money for drugs. Bizarrely, Moore always overlooked these betrayals and the ex-husband remained a permanent houseguest.

But Moore was becoming increasingly distanced from the foundations of his own past and career. With his wife and their entourage of her ex-husband, each other's children and numerous pets, he moved south of LA later that year, but gave hardly any of his old friends or colleagues his new phone number. Close friends who did see him noticed that he seemed to be in the grip of chronic melancholia, which was also tainted with a semi-permanent aura of distraction. At the beginning of 1995, Dudley's mindset was thrown further off-balance by the death of Peter Cook.

Although music was a constant and richly rewarding professional escape for Moore (he continued to play concerts and presented two entertaining and acclaimed musical television series), the lack of film work affected him badly. Moreover, his recent — and second — attempt to relaunch himself as a television sitcom star in the US had also failed. In 1994, CBS pulled *Daddy's Girls* off the air after just three episodes.

Things were beginning to look up, however, when he was offered a supporting role in a major film, Barbra Streisand's *The Mirror Has Two Faces*. But this instead turned out to be the final nail in the coffin of his film career, and pointed to the fact that something very serious was wrong with Dudley Moore.

As soon as shooting began, Dudley was clearly having problems. He could not remember his lines, even though his part was a small one. Streisand tried writing his lines on huge cue cards, but Moore still couldn't read them and turn in a realistic performance. Streisand tried to get to the root of the problem. Moore's chaotic home life and relationship with his wife was bound to affect his concentration, Streisand conceded. Dudley assured her that he would return, refreshed and refocused, for the following week's filming. Streisand tentatively nodded but was clearly not convinced. Before he could return, Moore learned that he had been fired from the film. (His replacement, ironically, was George Segal.)

Rumours began to abound, following Dudley's dismissal from *The Mirror Has Two Faces*, that he was a drunk, and his constant inebriation had caused him to forget his lines. Much of this was due to the public's strong identification of Moore with the role of Arthur, and is perhaps even a testament to how convincing he had been in that film. But the truth was that Moore was

Dad-to-be Dudley and Amy Irving.
Micki and Maude

not a particularly excessive drinker at this stage in his life — certainly not in Peter Cook's league anyway. His distracted mood and moments of inarticulacy were instead blamed by close friends on the stress of his personal life.

It is quite unsettling to revisit Moore's authorised biography (by Barbara Paskin), which, appearing in 1997, tried to explain away the odd behaviour that was later confirmed as the effect of a rare brain disease. Many times towards the end of the book, Paskin goes out of her way to underline how the pressure of moving home, tip-toeing in the volatile waters of his wife's mood swings, supporting her wayward ex-husband and struggling to meet all of his concert engagements was leaving Moore exhausted and unable to concentrate. But the list of depressing episodes she provides point to a startling mental decline, even without the benefit of medical hindsight. For example, soon after his dismissal from the Streisand film, Moore was pulled over by the police for swerving all over the road in his car. But he was not drunk. His commentary for a second series of a television show called *Really Wild Animals* was so confused and lifeless it had to be scrapped after he'd recorded it — even though he'd been reading it from a script. And on a reunion concert tour with Liza Minnelli in 1996, Dudley's jokes "fell flat" and were "punctuated with long pauses while he tried to conjure up some witty repartee that would pull the audience over to his side".

It was clear that Dudley was projecting just a shadow of his former glory; he seemed to be stuck in a vicious circle of failure, new hope and then new humiliation.

To add to this dispiriting confusion and loss of artistic grip, Dudley also began to experience heart problems; he underwent open heart surgery in 1998. In the following months, it was reported that he had suffered a series of strokes. Eventually, the cause of many of his recent problems was diagnosed — Dudley was suffering from progressive supranuclear palsy (PSP), a rare, degenerative and incurable brain disease.

Throughout these tormented times, Dudley only had his music as a rewarding outlet for his passions and ambitions. The greatest tragedy of his final years was that his illness also robbed him of this ability. As the inevitable effects of the PSP began to take their toll — symptoms included balance difficulty, rigidity in the limbs, slowness of movements, loss of co-ordination of eye movement, memory problems and slurred speech — Dudley was forced to give up his LA lifestyle. He split with Nicole and moved in with his close friend and long-time musical collaborator, Rena Fruchter, who lived more modestly in New Jersey with her husband. He became, essentially, their patient. It was clear that his condition, while leaving him — all the more tragically — intellectually alert, would soon leave him physically incapable of doing anything for himself.

Dudley made his condition public in 1999. In an interview for Barbara Paskin ('I'm Not Waiting to Die,' *The Times*, October 20, 1999), Dudley revealed the shocking reality of living with PSP. "In itself," Paskin reported, "PSP is not fatal, but as the disease gets worse, the difficulty in swallowing often leads to patients dying from choking on food, or contracting pneumonia when liquids get into the lungs."

Dudley's life had now become a reclusive existence of watching videos and struggling through meals. Fruchter and her husband were rocks of support, but there was something tragically ironic about his relationship with his family. Having been neglected as a child, he was now alone in late middle age. He confessed in the interview to having no contact with his four-year-old son from his marriage to Nicole Rothschild, and having "no interest" in seeing Patrick, his grown-up son from his marriage to Tuesday Weld. "Neither Patrick nor Weld have made any contact with him since the announcement of his illness," Paskin wrote.

Dudley revealed that the illness had now "brought the curtain down on all aspects of his career". Most upsettingly, this included his beloved musical endeavours. "It's agonising," he said. "I just can't play the sounds I hear in my head. My fingers don't respond properly."

He was still lucid enough to record a television interview with Barbara Walters in November 1999, in which he spoke movingly about the state of his life. With some effort, he even cracked the odd joke. But his appearance the following year on a BBC *Omnibus* documentary was nothing short of

Blame it on the Bellboy

Dudley Moore (as Patch) and David Huddleston (as Santa) in the Toy Tunnel.
Santa Claus The Movie

heartbreaking. Unable to speak coherently, Moore's mumblings were clarified by subtitles or translated by friends. As he stumbled around, aided by Rena Fruchter, he did however manage to articulate some profound observations on his condition, which were all the more disturbing for their searing honesty and insight. "It's totally mysterious the way this illness attacks, and eats you up and then spits you out.... I cannot make peace with it because I know I am going to die from it," he said. "To be reduced to this insignificant version of myself is overpowering." The most distressing image from the programme saw Dudley listening intently to a favourite piece of music. As it built to a crescendo, the star was clearly struggling with emotion as the sounds washed over him, but instead of looking like passion, it came over as pain.

Dudley's last public appearance was in November 2001, when he received a CBE from Prince Charles. It was the final pitiful image of a ten-year decline. Grey and emaciated, his face locked in an emotionless frown, Dudley was confined to a wheelchair. He was asked whether he had ever imagined receiving such an honour. He could only articulate the word "No", in response.

On March 27, 2002, Dudley Moore died of pneumonia, brought on by his PSP. He was sixty-six.

[*Dudley Moore filmography p.149*]

Part 3: Final Acts

Mary Ure
Anger and After

In the late fifties, John Osborne and Mary Ure were the most fashionable married couple on the London theatre scene. Osborne's first play, *Look Back in Anger*, had exploded into the nation's consciousness in 1956, and in so doing released the Royal Court Theatre from the dusty manacles of post-war primness and propelled it into a new era of aggressive vitality. Although still anchored to the rigid, three-act principles of the very drawing room plays it appeared to challenge, *Look Back in Anger* was nevertheless revolutionary in terms of its lead character, Jimmy Porter — a disillusioned, under-achieving but articulate and vitriolic protagonist who came to define the generation of 'angry young men'.

Mary Ure consolidated her reputation playing the fairly thankless role of Jimmy Porter's long-suffering wife throughout the play's initial runs in London and on Broadway. But she had already been on her way to establishing a serious pedigree before the world had heard of John Osborne. In 1954, at twenty-one, she had impressed critics and audiences playing alongside the esteemed stage actor Paul Scofield in *Time Remembered*. A year later, she was Ophelia to Scofield's Hamlet, a performance that led the Hungarian-born British film mogul Alexander Korda backstage into her dressing room to offer her a three-picture deal on the spot.

As it turned out, Ure made only one film for Korda (*Storm Over the Nile* [1955]) before his studio collapsed, but as she returned to the stage for Osborne's play, her stardom was eclipsing that of most of her theatrical contemporaries. She promptly married Osborne and, before long, the film version of *Look Back in Anger* (1959) re-established her as a screen presence.

Her remarkable, sensual performance in Jack Cardiff's version of *Sons and Lovers* (1960) led to an Oscar nomination for Best Supporting Actress. At twenty-seven, blond and beautiful, the world was focusing growing attention on Mary, as was an up-and-coming stage and TV actor named Robert Shaw.

Mary Ure with Richard Burton.
Look Back in Anger

Ure and Shaw had begun their affair in 1959. At first, Ure was the star and Shaw was in the shadow. When they eventually moved in together, she bought the house because he could not afford it. But Shaw was a competitive, controlling presence. Acting together on stage in 1960 was the first and last time Shaw would take second billing to Ure.

In 1960, Ure became pregnant with Shaw's baby (one of nine he would eventually father by three women). She and John Osborne divorced and immediately Ure began a cycle of motherhood that was to consume the entire decade. Marrying Shaw, Mary seemed at first to turn her back on her growing stardom to settle for a life as a wife and mother who occasionally acted. Shaw was on the brink of international stardom himself by this time, his villainous turn as the blond killer in *From Russia with Love* (1963) finally breaking him into the mainstream and setting him up as a leading man in his own right.

But soon Ure was eager to resume her own career, much to Shaw's disapproval. He countered this by either getting her pregnant again or involving her, very much as second fiddle, in his own projects. In Shaw's first screen role as star, *The Luck of Ginger Coffey* (1964), Ure was relegated to the 'love interest'. In *Custer of the West* (1966), she was merely decorative. And their salaries served to underline this. In *Custer*, Shaw, as the lead, was paid $350,000 to his wife's $50,000.

As time went on, naturally, Ure's desire to have children as well as express herself in her career began to put a strain on the marriage, and on her sense of well-being. But it was hard not to be overshadowed by a man like Shaw, who was both a physically and intellectually imposing presence. Not only was he an actor of magnetic power and steel-eyed sexuality, he was also an accomplished novelist. By the end of the sixties he had penned four critically-acclaimed books, including *The Hiding Place*, *The Flag* and *The Man in the Glass Booth*.

After bearing four of Shaw's children, Ure had one more brush with stardom, supporting Richard Burton and Clint Eastwood in *Where Eagles Dare* (1969). Although this hokum was a world apart from treading the boards as Ophelia at the Lyric Hammersmith, it was a high profile return to the public eye, and the film's massive commercial success should have returned her to the kind of career she looked set for in the wake of her Oscar nomination for *Sons and Lovers*.

But in 1970, Shaw and his family were forced to leave Britain for tax reasons. Ure, still the subservient wife, dutifully began to set up the family home in Ireland, although her sense of resentment was growing. She had been a fairly heavy drinker since her marriage to John Osborne — a man whose apoplectic verbal rages, sneering contempt for the world around him and gluttonous appetite for extra-marital affairs would probably have driven any wife to the bottle. And being married to Shaw exacerbated this problem. Recently Shaw had taken up alcohol as competitively as he had embarked upon everything else, and, now ensconced in the rural isolation of their Irish estate, Mary began to keep up with him.

As Shaw's biographer and agent John French has written, before long the couple's marriage descended into a "series of drunken brawls". French comments how "Mary's reaction to alcohol was very different from her husband's. It made her fly into violent rages, and it made her want to take off all her clothes. She would scream a litany of abuse. Shaw had taken all her money, destroyed her career, made her into a housekeeper."

The promise of *Where Eagles Dare* quickly waned, and Mary resumed her housekeeping duties. Shaw also found his career faltering around this time. After a series of critical and commercial failures, his usual $300,000 fee was cut in half. In addition, he was finding it increasingly difficult to write.

In the early seventies, Shaw and Ure accepted a couple of roles as a 'team', firstly in the forgettable but not uninteresting Hollywood thriller *The Daughter* (aka *Reflection of Fear*; released in 1973) and on Broadway, as two of the three characters in Harold Pinter's latest play *Old Times*.

The Daughter further highlighted the fiscal inequalities that characterised the Shaw/Ure relationship and how steeply her profile had dropped. According to John French, Shaw was paid $100,000 and ten per cent of the profits for ten weeks' work on the picture, with $1,000 a week in expenses; Ure was paid $10,000 for seven weeks' work and had to stump up her own air fare. It was not, French comments, "a situation designed to improve her temperament or her feelings for her husband, who was only too happy to point out ... that her employment depended on him." To make things worse, *The Daughter* was critically lambasted and publicly ignored. It was to be Mary's last film appearance.

The run of *Old Times* was more her forte, but although the play was a critical hit, it was not the commercial success it had been in the West End. After it closed, Mary entered a period of steep personal decline. Although in the eyes of the public they were happily married, Mary and Robert were spending more and more time apart. In private moments, she was violent and vociferous, accusing Shaw of an affair with his personal assistant (which turned out to be true).

Shaw's success in *The Sting* (1973) did not help Mary's growing instability. Her alcohol-induced rages became more frequent, as did her penchant for drunken exhibitionism. One night, French reports, Shaw awoke in their New York apartment to find that Mary had vanished. Fearing the worst, he went out to search the city for her. He found her walking naked alongside

It's a Broadway hit! Playwright John Osborne and wife Mary Ure arrive at London Airport after "Look Back in Anger's" New York success

***Lilliput** magazine, late fifties, reporting John and Mary's triumphant homecoming.*

the edge of Central Park.

In periods of sobriety, however, Mary was keen to go on working. She accepted a part in another stage production, *Love for Love*, which opened in Philadelphia in September 1974. However, barely two months into the run she was fired — officially for being "unable to communicate with the audience". Stunned, she began a campaign for unfair dismissal.

As the arbitration dragged on, Mary returned to England to accept another role in the West End in a thriller called, fashionably, *The Exorcism*. The play's first night was to be April 2, 1975.

Rehearsals went well, as did the preview performances, but offstage Mary's reliance on drink and a variety of prescription pills was as serious as ever. And her marriage to Shaw was now disintegrating fast. The night before *The Exorcism* opened was typically fraught, with Mary engaged in a drunken, violent slanging match with Shaw — who was staying with her in London while he filmed the caper *Diamonds* (1975) — followed by a pill-induced sleep. This strenuous battle continued after her opening performance the next day, which nevertheless seemed to go down well enough.

After the 'first night' party, Ure returned home and resumed the hysterics with Shaw. In the early hours they got tired of arguing and Shaw left Mary in the living room. The next morning he noticed that she was still there, and that she had been sick, but he left her to film a scene for *Diamonds* at the nearby studios. When he returned mid morning, Mary was in the same position, cold, lying in her own dried vomit.

It did not go unnoticed in the tabloids that Mary Ure had died 'mysteriously' after the first night of a play called *The Exorcism*. Lurid stories that followed the news of her death described how the theatre itself was exorcised the very next day. But for those who knew Mary well in her final years, her death was not so mysterious. Mary had, after all, been spiralling downwards, personally and professionally, for two or three years. Sooner or later, something had to give.

The coroner's report two weeks later concluded that Mary had choked to death after a lethal combination of alcohol and sleeping pills, although it was a mixture she had taken "in small repeated doses rather than the massive dose one associates with deliberation". *The Exorcism* resumed with an understudy in her role, while Mary, at forty-two, was consigned to that long list of show business casualties that cites booze and barbiturates as the cause of their demise.

Such was the state of their marriage that, after finding Mary dead, Robert Shaw informed the relevant authorities and then returned to the *Diamonds* film set for some afternoon shooting. Soon after, he went on to marry his secretary, and fathered another child. But it is fair to say that the numbing effect of Mary Ure's death may have blighted the rest of Shaw's life. Despite the massive success he was soon to have with *Jaws* (1975), he descended quickly into more pronounced alcoholism and chronic disillusionment. He seemed to care less and less about the film roles he took, and he would never resume his writing career. Robert Shaw himself died, only four years later, at the age of fifty-one.

[*Mary Ure filmography p.150*]

Vivien Merchant

Betrayal

Young Ada Thomson, it has been said, was a mass of contradictions. She had the face of a dowdy nanny, but the body and poise of an erotic model. She had an instinctive grasp of serious acting but contempt for all things intellectual.

She was rooted in the blunt reality of her humble Manchester upbringing but took the glamorous Vivien Leigh as her role model. And although, as a gifted, versatile performer, she could lend herself equally to light comedy and serious tragedy, she became professionally and emotionally dependent on her the work of her playwright husband.

Ada Thomson had already become Vivien Merchant when she first met Harold Pinter. They had crossed paths briefly as members of the legendary actor-manager Sir Donald Wolfit's company in 1953, but it was at Bournemouth rep in 1956 that they fell in love. Vivien, having been on stage since the age of fourteen, was something of the company star, a professional, jobbing actress able to meet the varied demands of a life in rep. Michael Billington, in his biography of Pinter, has called her "the epitome, in short, of the theatrical pro".

Pinter, by contrast, was in her shadow at this time. Acting under the name David Baron, he fluctuated between leading and supporting roles in the weekly treadmill of old standards, bedroom farces and Agatha Christie thrillers.

Pinter and Merchant married in September 1956. Immediately, it was something of an odd match. While onstage Pinter was reliable, professional and adept at the 'general purpose' roles required of him, offstage he was intense, outspoken and opinionated. He was also trying to hard to break through as a writer, penning plays and sketches that, with their surreal blend of comedy and menace and in their fractured use of sparse, ambiguous dialogue, were diametrically opposed to the kind of drawing room tosh he was touring provincial theatres with as an actor.

Merchant, however, was quite defiantly anti-intellectual, despite her rather bookish appearance. And behind her 'plain Jane' features and her vocal primness lurked an alluring eroticism. Her figure has been much commented on, and her outward appearance of mild repression only partly disguised a tactile, sensual and emotive performer. There is no doubt that this intriguing mix of middle class propriety and seductive sexuality appealed to the young Pinter. Not only that, it also began to define the way he wrote roles for women.

Pinter's first full-length play, *The Birthday Party*, was staged in London in 1958, when the writer was twenty-eight. It was — now the stuff of theatre legend — a resounding failure, closing after just a few days. However, the play's very ability to rub critics up the wrong way and confuse the audience led to the forging of allegiances in some intellectual and avant-garde circles, and Pinter found himself with a small number of influential supporters in the aftermath of *The Birthday Party*'s failure.

Pinter was nothing if not determined. The embarrassment of a flop willed him on further, and the next two years saw him engaged in a flurry of writing activity that produced *The Dumb Waiter* (1959), *The Hothouse* (1959), sketches and short plays for television and radio and, finally, *The Caretaker* (1960).

In complete contrast to *The Birthday Party*, *The Caretaker* was an overnight sensation. Now, Pinter and Merchant were the fashionable theatrical couple, and were lifted immediately out of their relative poverty. Yet, at the same time, cracks were beginning to show in their marriage.

Still, Merchant now entered into a golden period of her career. In the years immediately following *The Caretaker*, all of Pinter's major female roles were played by Vivien, and with great success — particularly notable were *The Lover* (1962) on television, and *The Homecoming* (1965) on stage. And these were not just roles written by the playwright to ensure his wife had a job. As Edna O'Brien commented, the women in Pinter's early plays were, more often than not, "illuminated" by Vivien. She went on: "It would be impossible not to interconnect the Vivien the person... with the stage presence who had flesh, blood and very good legs."

*Vivien Merchant with Ian Holm in the stageplay, **The Homecoming**.*

There must have been something of the actress, particularly, in *The Homecoming*, which initially left audiences gasping at its brutal power and blunt display of sexual manipulation. As the American wife of an English academic who chooses to become a whore in her husband's East End family home, Merchant conveyed an alluring, self-knowing fatality that powerfully mixed sexual ambiguity with emotional fragility and surface gentility. It was a performance that gave flesh to an explosive idea, and one that was vital to the impact of the play.

But, as Michael Billington points out, "the supreme irony is that the period when Pinter was creating some of his juiciest roles for Vivien also saw the beginning of the long, slow, painful disintegration of his marriage." Indeed, there had been tension between the actress and her husband at rehearsals for the stage production of *The Lover*, which Billington puts down to a "growing disparity between Pinter's sudden world fame and Vivien's more localised reputation as a highly accomplished actress". In addition, Pinter had begun an affair (with television presenter Joan Bakewell) in 1962 that was to last seven years.

If Vivien was coming to rely on her husband for the 'juiciest' roles on stage, she was at least beginning to make her mark in films on her own merit. Her screen debut, in *Alfie* (1966), was a finely judged, sympathetic performance

Vivien with Dirk Bogarde and Michael York. **Accident**

(as the recipient of a harrowing backstreet abortion) which led to an Oscar nomination for Best Supporting Actress. And it won her the British Film Academy 'Best Newcomer' award, which at thirty-seven may have seemed a little late coming. She followed this with a characteristically Pinteresque turn of icy sexuality and unspoken agenda in Joseph Losey's absorbing and enigmatic *Accident* (1967), scripted, of course, by her husband.

But the casting of Pinter's next play saw the writer expand his increasing emotional distance from his wife into the professional arena. In a move that struck a severe blow to Vivien, Pinter and his director Peter Hall offered the female role in *Landscape* (1969) to Peggy Ashcroft instead of her. Vivien may have outwardly taken the news in her stride, but it was the first artistic evidence of her husband's desire to 'move on', to separate himself from Vivien in more ways than one. Significantly, the actress never went to watch a performance of the play.

The marriage, nevertheless, soldiered on, and Vivien was back as one of the three characters in her husband's next play, *Old Times* (1971). She also gave another couple of memorable screen performances at this time. As Alec McCowan's wife in Alfred Hitchcock's British comeback *Frenzy* (1972), she was amusing in a small comic turn that revolved around her inability to marry her culinary ambition with her cooking skills (a role which brought her the Best Supporting Actress Award from the New York Critics Circle). In Sidney Lumet's interesting *The Offence* (1972), she suffered admirably and convincingly as the wife of Sean Connery's brutal, desensitised cop. Vivien followed this by committing her triumphant performance in Pinter's *The Homecoming* to film, in Peter Hall's 1973 version for producer Ely Landau.

But her life was about to fall apart, personally and professionally. In 1975, Pinter embarked on a relationship with Lady Antonia Fraser, a historical biographer and the wife of a Tory MP, a woman about as far removed from Vivien as it may have been possible to be. And this was no semi-secret affair. Within weeks he had confessed its magnitude to his wife and moved out of the marital home. Devastated, Merchant began a campaign of vindictiveness and retribution that was to fill yards of tabloid column inches for the duration of the summer. In an era when aristocratic divorces were still shocking, Vivien publicly named Lady Antonia as 'the other woman' in a calculated front page 'exposé' interview for the *Daily Express*, and she was not above making petty jibes at her husband's new lover, on one occasion criticising the size of her feet.

But despite her emotional desperation and scornful retaliation, Vivien could not stop the progression of Pinter's affair with Fraser, and the two set up home and made plans for marriage. Vivien, shaken, continued working but the stage roles became intermittent and the films dried up altogether. Although more than capable of taking on roles outside her husband's plays, it was as if the withdrawal of his creative safety net had left her foundering. Since the early sixties, Vivien's reputation had come to rely on her husband's talent, despite her sporadic successes for other writers and directors. With Pinter gone, she slid into professional laziness and, before long, a drinking problem was to further hamper the progression of her career.

Pinter and Merchant were finally set to divorce in October 1980, and the playwright set a date to marry Fraser immediately after the papers had been signed. Vivien however did everything "to make life difficult right up to the last moment" and refused to sign the divorce papers in time for the wedding to take place. Pinter and Fraser ended up having to have their wedding reception two weeks before the official ceremony, which Michael Billington calls "a small vindictive triumph for the disgruntled Vivien".

But if this was a triumph, then it was certainly her last one. After the final severance of ties with her husband, Vivien only lived for two more years. She fell deeper into alcoholism and developed a reputation for unreliability, which effectively closed the remaining doors on her acting career. The *Daily Mail*'s theatre critic Jack Tinker recalled seeing her towards the end of her life acting in a revival of one of her ex-husband's plays, in which she was "nervous and hesitant". And in true *Daily Mail* style, Tinker noted how "not a female in the audience" could fail to register how much she'd let her figure go.

"No one who saw her," he went on, "bloated and tremulous ... could fail to recognise the sadly prophetic symptoms of a woman collapsing under her own sense of wrong."

It also came to light later that, during these final years, Vivien had tried to join the controversial suicide group Exit, but had been turned away on account of having too much to live for. Vivien did not agree. "In her wildest fantasies she seemed to believe that Pinter was still in love with her," commented one of her friends. The fact that he wasn't was a cross that she could never learn to bear. On October 3, 1982, Vivien Merchant died after a short illness brought on by chronic alcoholism. She was fifty-three. Jack Tinker titled his *Daily Mail* tribute to her "The Woman who Died of a Broken Heart".

Although Vivien had been provided for comfortably enough in the years following her split from Pinter, nothing, commented her legal adviser, "could stop her from drinking herself to death." He added: "I think she could never quite accept, despite the divorce, that she wasn't Harold Pinter's wife."

Pinter himself has faced some blame for Vivien's decline in her last years. But he did his best to support her after their split, and always eschewed the vindictive point scoring that Vivien herself often went in for. "The pity of it," Pinter has said of Vivien Merchant, "is that her reputation as an actress became tied up with my work, but it didn't need to … [P]art of the problem was that she was a pretty solitary person. She had very few women friends. She also no longer had the desire to act. She had become very possessive and very dependent. It was all very sad."

[*Vivien Merchant filmography p.150*]

Jill Bennett

Love and Death

When Jill Bennett came into his orbit in 1965, playwright John Osborne was an established force in the theatre. The years that followed the explosion that was *Look Back in Anger* in 1956 had seen him transcend the 'angry young man' label with a series of plays that surpassed *Look*'s blunt aggression and left impressions on the English theatre that resonate to this day — *The Entertainer, Epitaph for George Dillon, Luther, Inadmissible Evidence*. His involvement in the development of New Wave British cinema was no less impressive. With theatre director Tony Richardson he helped to create Woodfall, arguably the most important British film production company of the sixties. Woodfall was responsible for a slate of films that revolutionised 'adult' British cinema. It brought to the screen censor-challenging and socially-probing screen versions of stage successes such as Osborne's own *Look Back in Anger* (1959) and *The Entertainer* (1960), as well as Shelagh Delaney's *A Taste of Honey* (1961) and Alan Sillitoe's short story *The Loneliness of the Long Distance Runner* (1962). It produced the most ground-breaking film of its era: *Saturday Night and Sunday Morning* (1960). And, in *Tom Jones* (1963), it created a playful, bawdy, colourful postmodern epic that took Hollywood by storm and was showered with international awards (including the Best Picture Oscar).

By the mid sixties, actress Jill Bennett was also something of a veteran of stage and screen. She'd still been in her late teens when she had made her debut in Stratford-upon-Avon in the forties (although her actual birth date was later questioned, by Osborne and others); by 1950 she was acting with Laurence Olivier in the West End. Poised, pretty and exquisitely presented, Bennett's elfin appearance seemed to combine a feminine vulnerability with a peculiarly masculine aura, and her onstage presence was striking. In 1952, the film director John Huston noticed her, and immediately made room for her in his already fully-cast film of *Moulin Rouge.*

During this time, Bennett had also become drawn to her first theatrical powerhouse lover, the stage and screen actor Sir Godfrey Tearle. Tearle was more than forty years her senior, but she fell headlong in love with him nonetheless, and became his live-in partner. When he died in 1953 (aged sixty-nine), the actress entered a prolonged period of grieving for the relationship that she later claimed she'd never got over. Still, her career continued apace, although the notable stage roles were never quite matched on the screen. She hovered in the background of *Hell Below Zero* (1954) and Vincente Minnelli's Van Gogh biopic *Lust for Life* (1956). She made more of an impression in Joseph Losey's *The Criminal* (1960), but, as Stanley Baker's cuckolded moll, wailing through the film in a permanent state of semi-hysteria, that performance doesn't stand up today.

But the stage successes continued, and in 1965 the director Anthony Page recommended Bennett to Osborne for the role of Countess Sophia Delyanoff in the author's latest production, *A Patriot For Me*. Osborne recalls being somewhat reluctant to use her (although he would say that); nevertheless, it marked the beginning of a ten-year relationship that formed the best years of Bennett's career and the final cycle of glory for Osborne. In just a few scenes, Bennett made her mark on *Patriot For Me*, and the success of the play seemed to re-invigorate an increasingly apathetic Osborne. And during the play's run, Page, its original director, has noted that Osborne also began to "pursue her vigorously, asking her down continually for the weekends to the country, where he was living with Penelope Gilliatt". Soon, the actress and the writer were an item — Osborne ended his marriage to critic Gilliatt; Bennett had already split from then-husband Willis Hall.

Bennett took centre stage for Osborne's *Time Present* in 1968, and this became the first real high point of their personal and professional collaboration. Among other accolades, the role won Bennett Best Actress awards from the *Evening Standard* and the Variety Club. That same year, she appeared in the effective, but sadly little seen, screen version of *Inadmissible Evidence*, and then married Osborne at Chelsea Register Office.

Her film career trundled along; the roles onscreen were mostly supportive and never scaled the heights of her success in the theatre. But she popped up in some interesting places: *The Nanny* (1965), *The Charge of the Light Brigade* (1968), *Julius Caesar* (1970). On the London stage, however, she helped assure the success of her husband's *West of Suez*, and, in 1972, she had what was probably her finest hour in his adaptation of Ibsen's *Hedda*

Gabler. Of this role, Anthony Page has commented: "...she never stopped shaping the part with the humorous down-to-earth persistence, intelligence and inspiration of the real artist that she could be. After seeing the performance, John Guare, the American playwright, told me that she had revealed Ibsen to him in a way that no other actor had."

But by this time, things were beginning to turn sour at home. Alcohol and apathy had gripped Osborne; the spark between the couple had gone. The marriage fell apart (it was finally dissolved in 1977). Bennett was in her mid forties (or older) by then. But the good roles kept coming, at least for a while. On stage: revivals of Strindberg's *Dance of Death* and Rattigan's *Separate Tables*. Later, she was a powerful Gertrude to Jonathan Pryce's *Hamlet*. On screen (television, at least) she had her finest role in front of a camera in Alan Bennett's *The Old Crowd* (1979). She also turned up in *Full Circle* (1977), *For Your Eyes Only* (1981) and was memorable in Lindsay Anderson's badly misfiring *Britannia Hospital* (1982). Still, there is an element of truth in John Osborne's later claim that "after we separated ... she was consigned to lesser parts"; certainly, the Golden Years of 1965–72 were never recaptured.

Jill kept busy as the eighties began, although, more and more, there was a journeyman air to the way her career was developing, despite the occasional 'big classical' role and the fact that she could display the talent of a theatrical dame when she felt up to it. But as she got older, and as her unique looks started to sag, she seemed to find it increasingly difficult to paper over the cracks of her private life with the glamorous abandon of being an actress. Certainly, she remained waspish, playful and mercurial in the company of friends, but those who knew her well saw that her resilience and independence were being tested in the lonely post-Osborne years. Given to self-professed bouts of 'Celtic gloom' (she was half Scottish, although she was born in Malaysia), she indulged in a champagne and caviar lifestyle more to 'deaden the pain' than to wallow in glamorous excess. After her death, *The Guardian* obituary perceptively stated that "she felt what she regarded as the failures of her private life very painfully." Like her tragic friend Rachel Roberts, Jill was childless at fifty. Outwardly, this seemed in keeping with her sociable lifestyle. In truth, she had been stung by losing two pregnancies during her marriage to Osborne, and by the assertion soon after that she would never be able to have children.

In the late eighties Jill began an affair with a multi-millionaire stockbroker, Thomas Schoch. It seemed an easy, casual relationship, his sturdy sensibility complementing her alluring tempestuousness. But when his interest in the affair began to wane, the actress could not shake the feeling of loss and dejection, despite having admirably weathered similar situations before. Rather than move on, Jill appeared to be clinging to Schoch, and unable to let go. In December 1989, Schoch left her to spend Christmas with his wife and family; from that point on, Jill Bennett went into steep decline.

Her career, however, was still fairly robust. She had just completed what was to be her last film role, in *The Sheltering Sky* (1990) for director Bernardo Bertolucci. And although this turned out to be a somewhat thankless part

— loud, shrill, shrewish — it was certainly high profile enough to be noticed internationally. But such potential rewards did not alleviate Jill's personal suffering. Cal McCrystal, in a profile of the actress written shortly after her death, noted that in the months following December 1989, "something close to despair set in. Nobody could arrest what was turning into inexorable decline. Anti-depressant pills failed. Her addiction to half-bottles of champagne, which she kept refrigerated at the foot of her bed, brought only brief escape."

In August 1990, the actress took an overdose; she was found in time to have her stomach pumped, and she seemed to make a physical recovery. More than likely, this episode was intended to devastate her retreating

Jill Bennett

lover, although it was no half-hearted suicide attempt. Even so, John Osborne later spoke, uncharitably of course, of "how carefully she knew the practical drill of suicide and how many times she rehearsed it". The suicide bid did alert her estranged lover nonetheless; he made a tentative reappearance in her life, but it was not to refuel their affair.

The subsequent months were not lifted by her rescue from death or by the courteous (if detached) concern of her ex-lover. Visiting a friend for dinner in September 1990, she talked again of the practical aspects of suicide, and how one goes about it. That same month, other friends noted how she had all but confined herself to bed (in Schoch's house in Gloucester Walk, Chelsea), without the energy to dress or make up. A friend later commented: "She was desolate. She still felt that her relationship with Thomas might resolve itself, if only he would come back and say a few friendly words."

Jill Bennett was still at her ex-lover's house when, on October 5, 1990, her secretary found her dead in bed. She had taken another overdose. Six weeks later, the Westminster Coroner concluded that she had "committed suicide in a state of depression after the break-up of a love affair". The post-mortem examination revealed that she had taken far more than the normal therapeutic dose of quinylbarbitone. Jill was said to be fifty-nine; although some have

*Jill in **Hell Below Zero** publicity shot.*

speculated that her real age was more like sixty-three. In her will, the actress left most of her estate (£596,978) to Battersea Dogs Home.

Two years after her death, Jill's ex-husband John Osborne caused something of a stir by annihilating her character in the second volume of his autobiography, *Almost a Gentleman*. He begins by opining that Jill "was a woman so demoniacally possessed of Avarice that she died of it". Her suicide, he writes, was a "final, fumbled gesture, after a lifetime of glad-rag borrowings, theft and plagiarism", but also "one of the few original or spontaneous gestures in her loveless life". He goes on — calling his ex-wife 'Adolf':

"How do I know that Adolf didn't intend to kill herself? Very simple. Her body contained hardly a trace of alcohol. She was relying on someone 'coming in on her' sufficiently comatose for a good night's sleep but not enough to feel the brush of angels' wings." On her bequest to the dogs' home, he wrote: "It was the most perfect act of misanthropy, judged with the tawdry, kindless theatricality she strove to achieve in life. She had no love in her heart for people and only a little more for dogs." And his final words on the subject of his ex-wife: "I have only one regret remaining now in this matter of Adolf. It is simply that I was unable to look down upon her open coffin and ... drop a good, large mess in her eye."

Not surprisingly, Jill Bennett's friends were aghast at the viciousness of Osborne's onslaught. Several rallied around to redress the balance. Anthony Page asserted her wit, kindness and gentleness, and highlighted how the bequest to the dogs home was the merely result of "a series of mistakes and legal entanglements worthy of Evelyn Waugh and Dickens". Richard Eyre recalled how she was "accessible and warm-hearted, wonderfully droll and naughty, very unlike an English actress..."

But it is curious that her demise unleashed such a passion in Osborne, and fuelled him to produce an attack that was arguably the best thing he'd written in ten years (the last good thing had been a prolonged attack on his mother, in his first volume of autobiography, *A Better Class of Person*). There is no doubting the horror of this spiteful diatribe, but was it fuelled by a howling truth? Cal McCrystal, in an early tribute, did write that the actress

With Graham Crowden and Malcolm McDowell. **Britannia Hospital**

was "bitter and unpardoning at the close of a magnanimous professional and social existence" — something that could be "deduced from her last written messages". Her final note to her last lover was believed to contain "a wish that her death by her own hand bring him no relief". Still, the actress was hardly in her right mind at this point in her life. And it is worth remembering that, by 1992, John Osborne was bitter, bile-soaked and bombastic; his voice had been strangled by nearly two decades of alcoholism and (considering his beginnings) professional underachievement.

Were it not for the tributes from her professional friends, the memory of Jill Bennett may well have been truly sullied by the powerful attack by Osborne. Indeed, his assertion that she was incapable of love, at least for another human being, could be seen to be underlined by the nature of her last will and testament. But one other thing calls Osborne's hatchet job into question. In 1983, thirty years after the death of her first lover Sir Godfrey Tearle, Bennett felt compelled to write a book on her liaison with the grand old actor. The result, *Godfrey: A Special Time Remembered*, is a sincere evocation of a poignant May-to-December love affair, infused with a pragmatic, unsentimental yet touchingly human streak of vulnerability. And in its opening lines, Bennett confesses:

"I never have got over the man I loved when I was very young... I didn't know ... that the four years we had spent together were going to affect my life for bad as well as for good. Much of what we shared was full of joy, but he still cast his long shadow across my future ..."

She went on: "The thorn that I've never managed and probably never wanted to dig out of myself is that after Godfrey died his affect on me did not. He looms heroic in my imagination. I am dazzled by him still."

Jill Bennett was in her fifties when she wrote this. She had since experienced a lifetime of joy and sorrow, success and failure. But in her last, self-imposed days of confinement, she was still re-running old films of Tearle's and shedding tears. Even then, thirty years older and wiser, the loss of love was still too powerful for her to endure.

[*Jill Bennett filmography p.150*]

Ian Hendry
The Nearly Man

When Ian Hendry died, few people really seemed to notice the loss or appreciate the tragedy of his life. It made the national papers, but not in any significant way.

Like many good British film actors, Hendry had suffered something of a downward spiral in his career during the 1970s, a decline that was exacerbated by personal problems such as divorce, alcoholism, bankruptcy and ill health. Consequently, he had faded, both in films and on TV, from potential stardom to B-list cameo roles and provincial theatre tours.

Such decline and under-use must have been particularly hard for Hendry and his fans to stomach, for he was a strikingly appealing and aggressively powerful actor who, in the sixties, very nearly made it big.

If it's any consolation, Hendry's name isn't likely to be forgotten by the hordes of cultists who champion TV's *The Avengers* (1961–69). Hendry as Dr David Keel and Patrick Macnee as Steed were the original avengers, seeking retribution for the murder of Keel's girlfriend. The first series ran throughout 1961 and was moderately popular, but the (then) ambitious Hendry decided to leave before a second series was produced. This may have been an early indication of the actor's bad luck — he was replaced by Honor Blackman, of all people, and the revamped *Avengers* skyrocketed into international TV history. Still, it is unlikely that Hendry would have been comfortable in what *The Avengers* became. His sights were set on serious film acting, on aggressive, gritty roles, and he knew he could do them.

On the big screen, Hendry made his first impression in *Live Now, Pay Later* (1962), a serio-comic programmer with satirical pretensions. As a salesman

Ian Hendry (right) with Michael Caine. **Get Carter**

dogged by personal problems, his role in this forgotten feature now seems like some kind of comic prophecy of his later career. *The Beauty Jungle* (1964) was probably Hendry's first good film: a sensationalised showbiz tale assembled with verve by Val Guest and performed with energy. Hendry was being groomed for star parts, to which he could easily have brought a fashionably dangerous presence. Raw, powerful, capable of both regional intensity and urbane machismo, with the right roles he could have held his own with the new wave of testosterone-fuelled British actors that was flooding the sixties.

By 1965, Hendry was catching the eye of important directors, although they invariably cast him in supporting roles. In Sidney Lumet's *The Hill* (1965), he spends the film shouting and barking at Sean Connery *et al* in a North African military prison; in Roman Polanski's remarkable *Repulsion* (1965), he is on the periphery of Catherine Deneuve's madness. Still, these respected films didn't really present the springboard that Hendry needed. Despite his rugged and virile appearance, he wasn't especially handsome and was losing his hair: these things may have kept Hendry away from nailing the high profile roles that he craved. Nevertheless, he continued to work steadily, turning up briefly in *The Sandwich Man* (1966), *Casino Royale* (1967), *The Southern Star* (1969) and *Doppelganger* (1969), and starring in TV's *The Informer* (1967). But then things started to go wrong.

By the end of the sixties, Hendry was enduring a turbulent marriage to the former family film star Janet Munro. Both husband and wife had taken to drinking, and the tempestuous and booze-soaked liaison was turning out to be mutually destructive. Although only in her thirties, Janet Munro's career had peaked ten years earlier when she was chosen from 500 auditionees and given a contract with Disney. She then appeared in *Darby O' Gill and the Little People* (1958) and *Swiss Family Robinson* (1960), before leaving Disney and appearing in *The Day the Earth Caught Fire* (1962). A number of forgettable films followed, and by 1970 she was yesterday's news.

Similarly, Hendry had grown bitter about his failure to secure the film star status that had appeared to be in his grasp. When Mike Hodges was casting *Get Carter* in 1970, he was considering Hendry for the lead role. That changed when Michael Caine, coasting on his first few years of international success, expressed an interest. Hodges jumped at the chance to have Caine on board, even though he'd "never thought that someone like Michael Caine would want to play such a shit".

Could Hendry have played Carter? In many ways, Hendry might have been better in the role. Hodges' initial concerns about Caine hit the nail on the head. Caine seems to be straining a little in the movie, despite all the praise for his tight-lipped, steely-eyed performance. Nastiness is just not something he does without effort. Hendry, on the other hand, would have let rip in the role. His inherent aggression, regret and bitterness, already exacerbated by drink, could have been channelled into a truly dangerous performance, one a shade more convincing than Caine's. But would *Get Carter* be remembered today if it wasn't for the presence of an established star like Caine? Probably not, but the film itself would have been none the worse for it.

So Hendry had to make do with a significant but nonetheless underexposed supporting role, that of Carter's chauffeur-outfitted nemesis, Eric Paice. And Hendry certainly didn't hide his displeasure at being eclipsed by Caine during the making of the film. "He was very jealous of Caine," director Mike Hodges has said. "When we rehearsed the [racetrack] scene, Ian arrived at Michael's suite in the hotel and he was pretty drunk, and it was just chaos. He was so vitriolic …" Hodges had to cancel the rehearsal. Caine knew from then to keep his distance. "I've always avoided drunks like the plague," Caine has said. "Ian wasn't a drunk, he was just a very heavy drinker." Still, when they played the scene before the cameras, "it was just perfect," said Hodges.

But one of *Get Carter*'s biggest flaws is its criminal under-use of great turns like Hendry and John Osborne. Both actors present brilliantly malevolent, snake-like characters, but are essentially confined to one scene each. *Get Carter* has great scenes, but it is too busy a film, and it looks like TV. It certainly wasn't lauded in its day, and only began to receive heated plaudits when it was embraced by the middle class lag magazines in the mid-nineties. Still, it has become the only film Ian Hendry is likely to be properly remembered for.

In 1971, Hendry was set to star, with wife Janet Munro, in a BBC TV series called *The Lotus Eaters*, about a bar-owning couple working on a Greek

Hendry with his feet up.

island. But before the cameras could roll, Munro pulled out, blaming the breakdown of her marriage to Hendry. The show almost had to be scrapped, but went ahead when a replacement for Munro, Wanda Ventham, stepped in. In the meantime, Munro and Hendry divorced.

The Lotus Eaters, broadcast in 1972, was a successful and respected series, with a characteristically bitter and boozy performance from Hendry. He clearly had a lot to draw on, but it was, essentially, his last significant work as a leading man. In December that year, Janet Munro died after choking on a cup of tea. She was thirty-seven,

In 1973, Hendry appeared in the sensational Vincent Price vehicle, *Theater of Blood*. This was one of his last career highlights, indulging in thespian sparring with the great Price and leading one of the most awesome British supporting casts of the seventies. Of course, Hendry is not much more than Price's comic foil here, but he brings a great dignity to the role — unsurprising, given that he started his professional acting career as a clown's stooge. That same year, Hendry also made *Assassin*, and gave a good performance in a lousy film. As an unemotional hitman, he gave an indication, perhaps, of what he could have brought to the role of Jack Carter.

With booze and health problems now dogging him, the mid seventies seem to present the disastrous turning point in Hendry's film career. While in 1975 he was supporting Jack Nicholson and Maria Schneider in Michelangelo Antonioni's *The Passenger*, 1976 saw him as 'Uncle Rodney' in a cheesy British

Hendry in **The Beauty Jungle**.

sex romp, *Intimate Games*. He stumbled through the rest of the seventies, and can be seen far into the background of *Damien: Omen II* (1978), *The Bitch* (1979) and *McVicar* (1980), but it's hardly worth looking for him.

In January 1980, Hendry was declared bankrupt, but managed to placate the taxman by securing gainful employment in a daytime soap for ITV, *For Maddie With Love*, co-starring Nyree Dawn Porter. Artistically, it was a pretty steep comedown from the film roles of the sixties, but it at least got Hendry out of a tight spot. Of the £43,385 he earned in 1980, mainly from the soap, £30,000 of it had to go to the Inland Revenue.

Screen work became more scarce for Hendry as the eighties got under way. In 1984, he surprised many by turning up in the TV soap *Brookside*. As drunken seadog Davy Jones, Hendry, clearly ill, looked startlingly old and ravaged, but it was good to see the gruff old aggression still in place. After a few nights he was gone again, clutching his duffel bag, tossing an empty liquor bottle over his shoulder as he stomped back to sea. All too brief, it was a memorable, booze-fuelled turn. Rather like the actor's life.

On Christmas Eve 1984, Hendry collapsed and was rushed to the Royal Free Hospital in London. He died shortly afterwards. The coroner would only confirm that the actor died of natural causes. He was fifty-three. And despite appearing in over thirty films and clearing up his problems with the Inland Revenue, he was almost penniless.

[Ian Hendry filmography p.151]

David Rappaport
Even Dwarves
Started Small

David Rappaport, at one time the most successful 'short actor' in the world, had the confidence, the talent, the ability and the looks to transcend his dwarfism and stand tall among his contemporaries and co-stars. This was true whether he was pitched against the stellar cast of *Time Bandits* or Harry Hamlin and Corbin Bernsen in TV's *LA Law*. And what's more, he knew it. So self-assured became David, he spent his adult life in denial of his dwarfism. For a well-adjusted dwarf functioning in the real world, there are some healthy aspects to this kind of mindset. But it wasn't quite so healthy for an increasingly rampant egomaniac, fuelled by drugs and immersed in the image-obsessiveness of the Hollywood Hills.

There were, of course, a number of novelty roles open to a successful 3'11" actor, on both sides of the Atlantic. Even before David's career had kicked off in Britain, a young American film director offered him the chance to sit in a metal case in the Tunisian desert and waddle about pretending to be a robot. But *Star Wars* didn't seem to have a lot going for it at the time, and David turned it down. And this seemed a fairly wise decision. After all, what kind of an actor would want to be encased in a tin box in blazing heat for weeks on end and not have a chance to say any lines or even show his face? Plus, the money was terrible. All George Lucas could offer to tempt his cast was a percentage of the profits. And everybody knew, in early 1977, that science fiction was dead in the water.

The role of R2D2, then, went to Kenny Baker, who subsequently made a fortune, but even so, one can imagine that David Rappaport did not regret his decision to turn it down. Even at the height of the first cycle of *Star Wars* mania, who would have recognised Kenny Baker in the street, even as a performing dwarf? And could you see Kenny Baker with his short arms around two LA supermodels, sipping champagne beside a crystal blue swimming pool on Beachwood Canyon? David Rappaport needed to be seen and appreciated. He needed to be the centre of attention. He had wit, verve and charisma — 'playing' R2D2 would have been anathema to him.

Instead, David concentrated on making it in his own way. Graduating Bristol University in 1970, he had begun his career as a primary school teacher (the kids were taller than him). But by the mid seventies, he was becoming more interested in performing to wider audiences than classes of seven-year-olds. He got involved in fringe theatre, and soon after Ken Camp-

David Rappaport. **Robin of Sherwood**

bell cast him as an 'anarchic dwarf' in his stage production *Illuminatus!* The noted director Peter Hall saw the show and invited the company to perform it at London's National Theatre. Subsequently, Hall cast David in his own production of *Volpone*. Within months, David had soared from the coat-tailed improvisation of a semi-professional revue to a significant role alongside Sir John Gielgud. And with it soared his ego.

By this time, David had moved to live in a squat complex in London's Freston Road, and there he got involved with the bizarre community of 'Frestonia'. When the squatters were threatened with eviction, they took the rather surreal and humorously British step of declaring themselves an independent state, thus creating Frestonia. Providing playful copy in a world crippled by recession and unemployment, Frestonia was given generous international press coverage; David himself was frequently interviewed in his capacity as Frestonia's 'Foreign Minister'.

Such a refreshingly odd and tongue-in-cheek 'performance' did not go unnoticed, and pretty soon David was being offered work by TV comedy producers. By the end of the seventies, he was a regular on Spike Milligan's BBC series *Q9* and the anarchic Saturday morning show, *Tiswas* (in which he gave a funny turn as 'Shades').

In 1981, Terry Gilliam cast him in his offbeat schoolboy adventure yarn *Time Bandits*. As Randall, the leader of a group of vertically challenged, renegade time travellers, David almost steals *Time Bandits* (fittingly, as his character is a thief), despite being dwarfed, literally, by a roster of international talent (Sean Connery, Shelley Duvall, Ralph Richardson, David Warner, John Cleese) and by a series of deceptively gargantuan, typically Gilliamesque set pieces. Brash, arrogant, deluded but endearingly dignified, Randall provides the film with some of its best comic moments, as well as lending Gilliam much of the 'novelty value' he strives to achieve in every scene.

Some have commented, however, that *Time Bandits* also saw the true beginning of David's spiralling ego problems. Behind the scenes, he was reportedly 'contemptuous' of the other small actors in the film, and refused to be grouped with them, both as a dwarf and a performer. He also annoyed them by demanding most of the close-ups. Terry Gilliam has commented that David thought he had got the job in *Time Bandits* "because he was a great actor and not because he was a great four foot actor. Now, there's a subtle difference there ...[He] always kept himself separate from the rest... There was a certain antagonism that was building up within the group." As it turned out, this was actually beneficial to the film, as Randall sees himself as a cut above the rest of the bandit gang, but it is portentous of the ego problems that came to dog David later in his career. Despite his talent and infectious sense of humour, he seemed to be holding onto a harmful self-delusion. It is not insignificant that all of David's friends were people of normal height. The actor was refusing to see that his height was an issue. In a perfect world, of course, it shouldn't have been, but this was show business. David commented revealingly in a later interview that: "I have done several parts now that don't call for small people ... I must be extra careful, because as soon as I do a part that's a bit tacky or a bit dwarfy, then I feel I've gone back a year or two."

Time Bandits, meanwhile, was one of the surprise hits of 1981, both critically and commercially, and saw Rap-

The Wizard publicity shot.

paport break into the mainstream, as far as he could. Offers for more of the same started to come in — medieval romps and fantasy films with an offbeat spin. Rappaport, true to form, chose the high profile, star-studded projects: *Sword of the Valiant* (1983), with Trevor Howard, Peter Cushing and, again, Connery, and *The Bride* (1985), with Sting and Jennifer Beals.

It was *The Bride* that fuelled David across the Atlantic. After its release, in search of real fame and fortune, he went to live in Hollywood. Not surprisingly, given the actor's nature, the sun-blessed, filofax lifestyle of LA seduced him immediately. Witty and lucid, he threw himself into rounds of 'breakfast meetings' and chat show appearances. And soon David secured a lucrative leading role in the CBS TV series *The Wizard*, an 'enchanting' show about a crime-solving toy maker. In a broadcast schedule dominated by the materialistic monoliths of *Dallas* and *Dynasty*, and the downbeat drama of *Hill Street Blues* and *Cagney and Lacey*, *The Wizard* was an instant cult hit, and immediately gave David the Stateside stature he had been looking for.

But *The Wizard* could not compete with the enduring strength of its TV rivals, and was cancelled after twenty episodes. Nevertheless, it had been an ideal launching pad for David in the US. In the wake of the series, he was offered regular guest spots in *Hooperman* and, significantly, *LA Law*, in which he played lawyer Hamilton Schuyler, aka 'Mighty Mouse'. And he was now enjoying the lifestyle of a star; an October 1986 interview in *Peo-*

Rappaport with Clancy Brown and Jennifer Beals. **The Bride**

ple Weekly described how he entertained visitors at his duplex apartment, drove a specially adapted VW Rabbit, socialised at Tramps and occasionally lunched with Rosanna Arquette.

But when he later moved to Beachwood Canyon, and its constant round of pool parties and barbecues, David also began to succumb heavily to drink and drugs, and his friends and colleagues began to notice the destabilising effect they were having on his already volatile personality. And despite his growing fame, David had not shaken the mantle of 'novelty guest star'. No further leading parts in major projects such as *The Wizard* were forthcoming; the actor had to be content with small roles, in both senses of the term.

Ian Parker, in a profile of David written a year after his death (*The Independent*, 4 May 1991), also highlights how the trappings of Hollywood stardom were exacerbating the actor's ego problems: "As a child, David had been cushioned from danger by his friends. Now he was cushioned again … by the illusions of stardom. And he seemed to be losing touch; he seemed to believe it was all real."

In 1989, David got involved with *Beyond the Groove*, a pop TV series project that was the brainchild of Eurythmics' Dave Stewart (not someone who has ever been known for the success of his screen ventures). It was during the making of this series that the actor's increasing mania and paranoia became apparent. David's behaviour with the show's director Roger Pomphrey was particularly alarming. According to Ian Parker: "David started making constant reference to Pomphrey's inexperience … Then he accused Pomphrey of trying to cut him with a razor blade, and then accused the production of risking his life with a flying television set." He also refused to stay in the same hotel as the rest of the cast.

On one occasion, when Pomphrey was trying to calm the actor down after a particularly savage outburst, David spat in his face. The extreme behaviour of a spoilt child is one thing, but David was now exhibiting signs of mania. The actor's brother has commented that, at this time, David was becoming "less and less his normal self".

By early 1990, David had grown sufficiently unstable to make an attempt on his own life. On March 5, he drove up to the infamous 'HOLLYWOOD' sign on Beachwood Drive (where troubled actress Peg Entwistle herself had achieved legendary fallen star status in 1932 by throwing herself from the top). Here he stopped his car, attached a hose to the exhaust pipe and fed it through the window. But before he succeeded in killing himself, the police were alerted and arrived in time to pull his unconscious body from the car. David was revived and taken to hospital.

Over the course of the next few weeks, the extent of David's mental instability became clearer. It is unlikely that the lack of work had driven him to despair. He had already secured a part in TV's *Star Trek: The Next Generation*. (Once again, of course, he was on board for his novelty value, sharing the sound stage with an assortment of half-Vulcans and humanoids.) Rather than simply being at a very low ebb, David confided to his agent that he had been hearing voices in his head. Whether exacerbated by drugs and alcohol or not, this seems a clear symptom of paranoid schizophrenia.

David's near-suicide episode made the papers, and rumours about his mental health began to circulate. Even so, after being discharged from hospital, he was able go to an LA store and order a gun. The growing speculation over his condition was clearly irrelevant to the licensed firearms dealers. Nevertheless, there was a fifteen-day waiting period before David could pick up the weapon.

It is a sad illustration of David's state of mind that, during this fifteen-day wait, he did not have second thoughts about his suicidal plan, nor try to get help or confide in his closest companions. Instead, he fired his psychiatrist and on May 1,1990 (when the fifteen-day waiting period was up) David picked up the firearm without the delay. He then drove home and left a note for his fiancée saying he was going out to walk the dog.

David went to Laurel Canyon Park, a popular spot for local dog walkers. He got out with the gun and positioned himself by a hedgerow. Some time later, he shot himself in the chest.

A day later, a dog walker went over to see what his dogs had discovered under the hedgerow in the park. There he found the thirty-eight-year-old star lying dead. Not recognising 'the world's most successful short actor', the dog walker called the police to report that he'd found the body of a tramp.

[*David Rappaport filmography p.151*]

Charlotte Coleman

Forever Young

In the first ten years of her career, in her television roles as a child star and adolescent actress, Charlotte Coleman showed a maturity and a versatility that became, sadly, less and less well-utilised as she got older. At eleven, her cherubic face became familiar to millions as one of the two child stars (the other was Jeremy Austin) of television's *Worzel Gummidge* (ITV 1979–81), a nicely-crafted rural children's series about the exploits of an unruly scarecrow, based on the popular books by Barbara Euphan Todd. As well as providing, arguably, a career-best role for ex-*Doctor Who* Jon Pertwee, this quaint, amusing and perfectly 'Sunday tea-time' series drew solid and endearing performances from Coleman and Austin as the scarecrow's young (human) friends. Saucer-eyed and well-mannered, Coleman in *Worzel Gummidge* was quite the 'girl-next-farm', all cardigans and wellies and protectively good intentions.

Before the final series of *Worzel Gummidge* ended, however, Coleman showed a completely different side to herself, as the wild-haired, post-punk, delinquent teenager Marmalade Atkins in the 1981 TV pilot *Marmalade Atkins in Space*. This in turn led to two series as the character (*Educating Marmalade*, ITV 1982–83; and *Danger — Marmalade at Work*, ITV 1984): the premise being that the unruly and frequently expelled schoolgirl was impossible to teach, and then impossible to employ. This rather annoying, one-note premise pretty much worked as a children's version of the annoying, one-note, 'anarchic' sitcom *The Young Ones*, which was at the same time gathering a excited college-age following on the BBC. Similarly, *Marmalade Atkins* was a huge popular success in its after-school slot, although perhaps more justifiably, because of its irreverence and two-fingered salute to some of the prim children's programmes that went before it (including, perhaps *Worzel Gummidge*).

The character of Marmalade Atkins may also have been closer to Charlotte Coleman in real life than the sensible part she'd previously played. During the series' run, the teenage Coleman herself went through a rebellious phase that saw her expelled from Camden High School, leave her family home and shack up with friends. But she also continued to act, turning up in TV plays, although to rather less effect.

Charlotte Coleman (left) with Geraldine McEwan.
Oranges Are Not The Only Fruit

But her most startling metamorphosis was yet to come. In the ground-breaking BBC mini-series, *Oranges Are Not the Only Fruit* (1989), Coleman — ginger-haired, hollow-eyed, passive and emaciated — was striking as Jess, secretly but more subversively rebelling against her religious fanatic mother by embarking on a lesbian affair. The role required Coleman, twenty-one but looking five years younger, to perform lesbian love scenes. For those brought up on *Worzel Gummidge* and *Marmalade Atkins*, it was a jolting display of the actress's depth and commitment.

Charlotte as Marmalade Atkins.

Oranges Are Not the Only Fruit was showered with international awards, Coleman herself being voted Best Actress by the Royal Television Society. And it should have consolidated her already impressive credentials and signalled the beginning of an important 'grown up' career. But strangely it didn't. Her next role, in the abortive sitcom *Freddie and Max*, did nothing for her, and the early nineties saw Coleman slipping into jobbing actress parts in films and on television.

She did regain some fashionability as Hugh Grant's platonic flatmate in *Four Weddings and a Funeral* (1994), where, as the tomboyish imp Scarlett, she made a lasting impression in the film's first scene, in which she runs through London, late for a wedding, sporting a jarring ensemble of spiky orange hair, dishevelled party frock and trainers. But in reality this was a pretty thankless role, the kind of 'harmless eccentric friend' that Richard Curtis likes to pepper his scripts with, and Coleman's oddball appearance seemed to be little more than a trippy composite of her Jess and Marmalade Atkins characters.

Although she received a BAFTA nomination for Best Supporting Actress for *Four Weddings ...*, Coleman found the effect of the role quite damaging, typecasting her as it did as a kooky comic sidekick. Nevertheless, she was rarely out of work after that, and continued to turn up in some interesting TV and film projects, such as *The Young Poisoner's Handbook* (1995), *Different for Girls* (1996) and back to nature with the rural sitcom *How Do You Want Me?* (BBC 1998–99).

As she entered her thirties, however, Charlotte was becoming tired of playing the impish girl-woman. Yet her physique seemed to dictate that

Charlotte with John Hannah. **Four Weddings and a Funeral**

these roles would always be offered to her. Frail, petite and ghostly, she cut a rather alarming figure with her boyish haircuts and her wildly mismatched children's clothes. Even so, Roderick Gilchrist, executive producer on *How Do You Want Me?* has commented that "she felt there was a huge gap in her life. That everyone else had moved on but she hadn't... She hungered to play mature; she kept getting juvenile."

Personally, Charlotte's life had been blighted by the death of her boyfriend (in a motorcycle accident) when she was nineteen, an event she never got over. She subsequently developed an eating disorder, and her fragility was exacerbated by her acute asthma.

Roderick Gilchrist remembers that "there were times when her birdlike body was so thin that she looked like an Oxfam orphan" and recalls seeing her at a racing event, after they'd worked together, frail and "hollow-eyed". "I encouraged her to join me in the paddock to present a trophy to a winning jockey," Gilchrist commented. "Her arms were so weak she could hardly pick up the silver cup."

Some time later, on November 14, 2001, Charlotte Coleman had an asthma attack that she was not strong enough to survive. Her mother found her dead in her London flat. She was thirty-three.

[*Charlotte Coleman filmography p.152*]

Sir Stanley Baker
The Outsider

Stanley Baker was never a fallen star — he was too down-to-earth and headstrong to ever again experience the hard times he had known as a boy. But towards the end of his life, and he only lived to forty-nine, he seemed to be washed up as an actor, perhaps largely because he resolutely refused to keep up with the times. Even in the early seventies, young audiences thought of him as a dinosaur. Today, most people younger than middle age have never heard of him, let alone remember him, and if they do, they are likely to confuse him with Stanley Baxter — a popular Scottish comedian with a penchant for impersonating the Queen.

Certainly, in comparison with the legend of his countryman and contemporary, Richard Burton, Baker is all but forgotten. Yet, in many ways Baker had a more effective on-screen presence than Burton, and, in retrospect, he seems to have contributed more to the British cinema of the fifties and sixties. Still, his achievements are rarely reassessed or celebrated today, while Burton's reputation grows ever stronger.

Baker was shrewd and intelligent without aspiring to intellectualism; he looked striking and imposing but was not conventionally handsome; he was famous and formidable, but never an international star. He brought a versatile dichotomy to British films of the time. On demand, he could be dependable or threatening, violent or peacemaking, intimidating or passive. And, in a cinema still dominated by middle class drawing room manners and received pronunciation, he stood alone as the antithesis to the polite English heroism of Noel Coward, John Mills, Michael Redgrave and Kenneth More.

In the early years of his career, Baker portrayed heavies, and his Welshness was often used to personify villainy. When he became a star, it came to symbolise a working class ruggedness. In his prime, Baker seemed to be the only leading actor in mainstream British cinema portraying Welsh protagonists at all: *Blind Date* (1959); *Eve* (1962); *A Prize of Arms* (1962). Richard Burton's characters, by contrast, were almost invariably English, or in some way 'international'.

Baker stood far behind Burton in terms of international appeal and perceived acting ability, but the similarities between the two men's lives and careers are considerable. Born in south Wales in the twenties, both were from hard, poverty-stained backgrounds. Both, as raw, undisciplined youths, were moulded into protégés by tirelessly paternal schoolmasters. And, with similarly imposing acting styles of controlled danger and virility, both had made significant impressions in film by the mid 1950s.

But where Burton was academic, Baker represented the uneducated.

Sir Stanley Baker.
Zulu

Where Burton became a celebrity with Hollywood trappings and paparazzi appeal, Baker remained subversive, abrupt and, in a British sense, parochial. And where Burton personified the paradox of a 'classical English' theatre actor prostituting himself in empty big budget spectacles like *Cleopatra* (1963) and pandering to the gossip columns with his sex life, Baker remained pragmatic, close-mouthed and down-to-earth. He never seemed to be part of the 'in crowd'.

It is interesting to note then that much of Baker's best work in British films was not done with British directors, but with fellow 'outsiders' — namely, the American Joseph Losey and South African-born Cy Endfield, both of whom were exiled to Britain from Hollywood in the wake of McCarthyism. Baker's films with Endfield were popular, commercial, lowbrow fodder that injected sensationalism and an earthy vibrancy into the ration-book staidness of British popular cinema of the time: *Hell Drivers* (1957), *Sea Fury* (1958), *Jet Storm* (1959), *Zulu* (1964), *Sands of the Kalahari* (1965). *Hell Drivers* is more akin to Hollywood pulp fiction than a product of fifties Britain. *Zulu* (which Baker co-produced with Endfield) was, of course, a massive commercial success, and made the actor an extremely wealthy man.

If Endfield's films brought Baker's leadership qualities to a wider audience,

Baker comforted by Susannah York. **Sands of the Kalahari**

Joseph Losey quickly proved that there was more to the actor than rugged heroics and dependable villainy. In *Blind Date*, *The Criminal* (1960) and *Eve*, Baker delivered powerful and finely shaded performances that added to his commercial appeal. Even Losey's more popular films were rarely as straightforward or as easy as Endfield's, and it was with Baker that the director began to refine the style that established his formidable European reputation in the sixties and seventies. *Accident* (1967) was perhaps the true revelation of their partnership. As a cynical, emotionally-crippled Oxford don, Baker handles the ambiguous subtleties of *Accident*'s spare script (by Harold Pinter) equally as well as the film's 'deeper' actors, Dirk Bogarde and Vivien Merchant. Playing against type, Baker is quiet, vindictive and pained — his clipped sentences are lined with loathing, greed and regret. It is a performance that suggests he could and should have gone on to tackle wider ranging performances as he matured.

But Baker was not one for moving with the times. A stubborn, old-fashioned, fairly humourless character, he claimed to be a socialist, but if he was it was definitely of the champagne guzzling, reactionary variety. Given his poverty stricken start in life, however, his headstrong determination to succeed in business and better his lot is understandable. But such qualities left him markedly out of place as the sixties ended.

In 1970, Baker was only forty-two, but he looked older than his years and he continued to avoid 'fashionable' projects. He wore his (toupeed) hair

Baker. ***Violent Playground***

short and was rarely seen wearing anything but a conservative suit. By then, he seemed to belong to the dour, monochrome Britain of the late fifties, to thick-ear crime thrillers, or to pedestrian action adventures. And he was still churning out the kind of *Boy's Own* hokums and dreary international espionage thrillers that defined that bygone era. The few times he did seem to let his hairpiece down — such as in *Perfect Friday* (1970), a routine heist comedy with nods to sexual liberation — he looked decidedly distracted.

Around this time, Baker and his wife turned their backs on Britain and surrendered to the golfing and culinary pleasures of Spain. Financially secure, Baker continued to reap the rewards of his business successes. His film company, Oakhurst, had produced *The Italian Job* in 1969, and he was a major shareholder in the Welsh independent television channel, Harlech TV (HTV). Compromising his acting with his Mediterranean exile lifestyle, however, saw a peripatetic

Baker appearing in a string of Europuddings that did nothing for his career as a performer. When he did return to Britain, it was to appear in dross like *Innocent Bystanders* (1972), or crummy HTV projects such as *Graceless Go I* (1974). During this time, the actor also made plans to set up a sequel to his career high point, *Zulu*.

At the beginning of 1976, at a party Baker was throwing, the actor gingerly showed his fingers to a guest, expressing some bemusement about their sudden stubby appearance. The guest bluntly announced that the stubbiness of his fingers meant that Baker had either cancer or serious heart problems. The following month, Baker was in hospital having a tumour removed from his lung. The operation appeared to have been a success, and Baker embarked on a punishing course of radiation treatment and chemotherapy.

But Baker's condition was terminal. He spent his last months in Spain wandering about his bungalow in his dressing gown, offering sporadic reminiscences to his visiting biographer, chastising his long-suffering wife, dining out when he had the strength and hacking up mouthfuls of phlegm on the lawn. Underneath his gown he was clad head to toe in a neck-high vest and long johns, as the cobalt treatment he had been given meant that exposure to the Spanish sun was likely to cover him in a rash of skin cancers.

By June it was found that the cancer had spread to his hip and he returned to London for a further prognosis. Whilst receiving treatment there, Baker, a friend of the then Prime Minister Harold Wilson, heard that he had been knighted for his services to the British film industry (and also, more than likely, because he was dying). He returned to Spain, but within days did not even have the strength to untie his pyjama cord. A specialist was flown out and informed the actor that he must return to England and better facilities. Before he could make the trip, Baker died on June 28, 1976, three months short of his fiftieth birthday.

In his last year, Stanley Baker had returned to his beloved Wales, appearing as 'Dad' in a BBC TV adaptation of *How Green Was My Valley* (1976). His ashes were scattered around his home town of Ferndale.

[*Sir Stanley Baker filmography p.152*]

Appendix

Selected Filmographies

Certain films are emboldened in the filmographies below. This is intended to denote — subjectively — the films that I feel are worth seeking out or — objectively — those that propelled the actors' careers to greater heights, albeit temporarily.

Carol White (1943–91)

1956	Circus Friends
1959	Web of Suspicion (*uncredited*)
	Carry On Teacher
1960	Beat Girl
	Never Let Go
	The Man in the Back Seat
	Linda
1961	A Matter of WHO
1962	Bon Voyage (*uncredited*)
	Ladies Who Do
	Village of Daughters
	Gaolbreak
1965	The Playground
1967	Prehistoric Women
	Poor Cow
	I'll Never Forget What's'isname
1968	The Fixer (US)
1969	Daddy's Gone A-Hunting (US)
1970	The Man Who Had Power Over Women
1971	Something Big (US)

Dulcima
1972   Up the Sandbox (US)
Made
1973   Some Call It Loving (US)
1976   Helter Skelter (US TVM)
1977   **The Squeeze**
1982   Nutcracker

Rachel Roberts (1927–80)

1953   Valley of Song
The Weak and the Wicked
The Limping Man
1954   The Crowded Day
1957   The Good Companions
1959   Our Man in Havana (*uncredited*)
1960   **Saturday Night and Sunday Morning**
1961   Girl on Approval
1963   **This Sporting Life**
1968   A Flea in Her Ear (France)
1969   Destiny of a Spy (US TVM)
The Reckoning
1971   Doctors' Wives
The Wild Rovers (US)
Baffled! (TVM)
1973   O Lucky Man!
The Belstone Fox
Alpha Beta
1974   Great Expectations (TVM)
Murder on the Orient Express
1975   Picnic at Hanging Rock (Australia)
1976   A Circle of Children (US TVM)
1978   Foul Play (US)
1979   **Yanks**
The Sorrows of Gin (US TVM)
When a Stranger Calls (US)
1980   The Hostage Tower (US TVM)
Charlie Chan and the Curse of the Dragon Queen (US)
1981   The Wall (US TVM)

Oliver Reed (1938–99)

1955   Value for Money (*uncredited*)
1958   The Square Peg (*uncredited*)
Hello London

1959   The Captain's Table (*uncredited*)
1960   The Angry Silence
        The League of Gentlemen (*uncredited*)
        Beat Girl (*aka* Wild for Kicks)
        The Two Faces of Dr. Jekyll
        The Sword of Sherwood Forest
        The Bulldog Breed (*uncredited*)
        His and Hers
        The Rebel
1961   No Love for Johnnie
        Curse of the Werewolf
        The Pirates of Blood River
1962   Captain Clegg
        The Damned
1963   Paranoiac
        The Scarlet Blade (*aka* The Crimson Blade)
        The Party's Over
        The Debussy Film (BBC TVM)
1964   The System (*aka* The Girl-Getters)
1965   The Brigand of Kandahar
1966   **The Jokers**
        The Shuttered Room (*aka* Blood Island)
1967   **Dante's Inferno** (BBC TVM)
        I'll Never Forget What's 'isname
1968   **Oliver!**
        Hannibal Brooks
1969   The Assassination Bureau
        Women in Love
1970   Take a Girl Like You
        The Lady in the Car with Glasses and a Gun/*La dame dans l'auto
        avec des lunettes et un fusil* (France)
1971   The Hunting Party
        The Devils
1972   Sitting Target
        Zero Population Growth (*aka* ZPG; Edict; The First of January)
        Age of Pisces
        Triple Echo
1973   Dirty Weekend/*Mordi e fuggi* (Italy)
        Days of Fury/*Il Giorno del furore* (Italy)
        Revolver (Italy)
        The Three Musketeers: The Queen's Diamonds
1974   Blue Blood
        The Four Musketeers: The Revenge of Milady
        Mahler
        And Then There Were None
1975   Tommy
        Royal Flash

Lisztomania (*uncredited*)

And Then There Were None (*aka* Ten Little Indians)

1976 The Sellout

The Great Scout and Cathouse Thursday (US)

Burnt Offerings (US)

Maniac (*aka* Assault on Paradise; Maniac; The Town That Cried Terror)

1977 The Prince and the Pauper (*aka* Crossed Swords)

1978 Tomorrow Never Comes (Canada)

The Big Sleep

The Class of Miss McMichael

1979 The Brood (Canada)

1980 Lion of the Desert (US)

Dr. Heckyl and Mr. Hype (US)

1981 The Great Quest (US)

Condorman (US)

Venom

1982 The Sting II (US)

1983 Masquerade (US TVM)

Two of a Kind (US)

Fanny Hill (Memoirs of a Woman of Pleasure)

Spasms (*aka* Death Bite) (US)

1985 Black Arrow (*aka* *La Flecha negra*) (Spain TV)

1986 Captive

Castaway

1987 Rage to Kill (US)

1988 The House of Usher (US)

Captive Rage

1989 The Adventures of Baron Munchausen (GB/Germany)

The Return of the Musketeers

1990 Treasure Island (US)

Panama Zucchero (*aka* Panama Sugar and the Dog Thief) (Italy)

1991 The Pit and the Pendulum (US)

Hired to Kill (US)

Prisoner of Honor (US TV)

1992 Severed Ties (US)

1995 Funny Bones

1996 *Luise Knackt Den Jackpot* (Germany)

Superbrain Der Bankraub Des Jahrhunderts (Germany)

The Bruce

Russisch Roulette (Germany)

The People vs. Larry Flynt (US)

1999 Parting Shots

2000 **Gladiator** (US)

Diana Dors (1931–84)

1946	The Shop at Sly Corner
1947	Holiday Camp
	Dancing with Crime
1948	Oliver Twist
	The Calendar
1949	Here Come the Huggetts
	Vote for Huggett
	It's Not Cricket
	A Boy, a Girl and a Bike
	Diamond City
1950	Dance Hall
1951	Lady Godiva Rides Again
	Worm's Eye View
1952	The Last Page
	My Wife's Lodger
1953	The Weak and the Wicked
	Is Your Honeymoon Really Necessary?
	It's a Grand Life
	The Great Game
1954	The Saint's Return
1955	Value for Money
	A Kid for Two Farthings
	An Alligator Named Daisy
	Miss Tulip Stays the Night
1956	**Yield to the Night** (US title: The Blonde Sinner)
	I Married a Woman (US)
	The Unholy Wife (US)
1957	The Long Haul (US)
	La ragazza del palio/The Girl Who Rode in the Palio (Italy)
1958	Tread Softly Stranger
1959	Passport to Shame
1960	On the Double
	Scent of Mystery (US)
1962	Mrs Gibbons' Boys
1963	West Eleven
1964	Allez France
1966	The Sandwich Man
1967	Berserk!
	Danger Route
1968	Hammerhead
1969	Baby Love
1970	There's a Girl in My Soup
	Deep End (West Germany/US)
1971	Hannie Caulder
	The Pied Piper

1972   Every Afternoon
       The Amazing Mr. Blunden
1973   Nothing But the Night
       Theatre of Blood
       Steptoe and Son Ride Again
       Craze
       From Beyond the Grave
1974   The Amorous Milkman
       Swedish Wildcats
       The Groove Room
       Bedtime with Rosie
       Three for All
1975   Adventures of a Taxi Driver
1976   Keep It Up Downstairs
1977   Adventures of a Private Eye
1979   Confessions from the David Galaxy Affair
1984   Steaming

Mary Millington (1945–79)

As Mary Maxted:
1975   Eskimo Nell
       Erotic Inferno
       I'm Not Feeling Myself Tonight
As Mary Millington:
1976   Intimate Games
       Keep It Up Downstairs
1977   Come Play With Me
1978   The Playbirds
       What's Up Superdoc?
1979   Confessions from the David Galaxy Affair
       Queen of the Blues
       The Great Rock'n'Roll Swindle (*cameo*)

Tony Hancock (1924–68)

1954   Orders Are Orders
1960   **The Rebel**
1962   The Punch and Judy Man
1965   Those Magnificent Men in Their Flying Machines (US/Italy/
       France)
1966   The Wrong Box

Richard Beckinsale (1947–79)

1972	Rentadick
	The Lovers!
1974	Three for All
1976	Last Summer (TVM)
1979	**Porridge**

Peter Sellers (1925–80)

1951	Penny Points to Paradise
1952	Down Among the Z Men
1954	Orders Are Orders
1955	John and Julie
1956	The Ladykillers
1957	The Smallest Show on Earth
	The Naked Truth
1958	Up the Creek
	tom thumb
1959	Carlton-Browne of the F.O.
	The Mouse That Roared
	I'm All Right Jack
1960	**Two-Way Stretch**
	The Battle of the Sexes
	Never Let Go
	The Millionairess
1961	Mr Topaze (*also directed*)
1962	**Only Two Can Play**
	The Waltz of the Toreadors
	Lolita
	The Dock Brief
1963	**The Wrong Arm of the Law**
	Heavens Above
	The Pink Panther
1963	**Dr Strangelove, or How I Learned to Stop Worrying and Love the Bomb**
1964	The World of Henry Orient (US)
	A Shot in the Dark
1965	What's New, Pussycat? (US)
	The Wrong Box
1966	After the Fox
1967	Casino Royale
	Woman Times Seven (US/Italy)
	The Bobo
1968	**The Party** (US)
	I Love You, Alice B. Toklas

1969   The Magic Christian
1970   Hoffman
1971   There's A Girl in My Soup
1972   Alice's Adventures in Wonderland
       Where Does It Hurt? (US)
1973   The Optimists of Nine Elms
       Soft Beds, Hard Battles
1975   The Great McGonagall
       The Return of the Pink Panther
1976   Murder By Death (US)
       The Pink Panther Strikes Again
1978   Revenge of the Pink Panther (US)
1979   The Prisoner of Zenda (US)
       Being There (US)
1980   The Fiendish Plot of Dr. Fu Manchu (US)

Charles Hawtrey (1914–88)

1922   Tell Your Children (*uncredited*)
1923   This Freedom (*uncredited*)
1933   The Melody Maker
1936   Sabotage
       Well Done, Henry
       Cheer Up (*uncredited*)
1937   **Good Morning, Boys**
1939   Where's That Fire?
       Jailbirds
1941   **The Ghost of St. Michael's**
1942   **The Goose Steps Out**
       Much Too Shy (*uncredited*)
       Let the People Sing
1943   Bell-Bottom George
1944   A Canterbury Tale
1945   Ten Year Plan (*uncredited*)
       Dumb Dora Discovers Tobacco (*short; director only*)
       What Do We Do Now? (*short; director only*)
1947   The End of the River
       Meet Me at Dawn (*uncredited*)
1948   The Story of Shirley Yorke
1949   Passport to Pimlico
       Dark Secret
1950   Room to Let
1951   The Smart Aleck
       The Galloping Major
1952   You're Only Young Twice
       Hammer the Toff

Brandy for the Parson (*uncredited*)
1954 To Dorothy a Son
Five Days
1955 As Long as They're Happy
Simon and Laura (*uncredited*)
March Hare
Man of the Moment
Jumping for Joy (*uncredited*)
1956 Timeslip
Who Done It?
1958 I Only Arsked!
Carry On Sergeant
1959 Please Turn Over
Carry On Teacher
Carry On Nurse
1960 Inn for Trouble
Carry On Constable
1961 What a Whopper!
Dentist on the Job
Carry On Regardless
1963 Carry On Cabby
Carry On Jack
1964 Carry On Spying
1965 Carry On Cleo
1966 Carry On Cowboy
Carry On Screaming
1967 The Terronauts
Carry On Follow That Camel
Carry On Don't Lose Your Head
1968 Carry On Up the Khyber
Carry On Doctor
1969 Zeta One
Carry On Camping
Carry On Again Doctor
1970 Carry On Up the Jungle
Carry On Loving
1971 Carry On Henry
Carry On At Your Convenience
1972 Carry On Matron
Carry On Abroad

Benny Hill (1924–92)

1956 Who Done It?
1960 Light Up the Sky!
1965 Those Magnificent Men in Their Flying Machines (US/Italy/France)

1968   Chitty Chitty Bang Bang
1969   The Italian Job
1971   The Waiters (*short*)
1974   The Best of Benny Hill

Terry-Thomas (1911–1990)

1947   Brass Monkey
1948   A Date with a Dream
1949   Melody Club
          Helter Skelter
1951   Cookery Nook (*short*)
1952   The Queen Steps Out (*short*)
1956   **Private's Progress**
          The Green Man
          Brothers in Law
1957   Lucky Jim
          Blue Murder at St. Trinian's
          The Naked Truth
          Happy is the Bride
1958   tom thumb
          Carlton-Browne of the F.O.
1959   Too Many Crooks
          School for Scoundrels
          I'm All Right Jack
          That's Odd (*short*)
1960   Make Mine Mink
          His and Hers
1961   A Matter of WHO
          Bachelor Flat (US)
1962   Operation Snatch
          Kill or Cure
          The Wonderful World of the Brothers Grimm (US)
1963   The Mouse on the Moon
          It's a Mad, Mad, Mad, Mad World (US)
          The Wild Affair
1964   **How to Murder Your Wife** (US)
1965   Strange Bedfellows (US)
          Those Magnificent Men in Their Flying Machines (US/Italy/France)
          You Must Be Joking
1966   Our Man in Marrakesh
          The Sandwich Man
          The Daydreamer (US)
          Munster, Go Home! (US)
          Se tutte le donne del mondo... (US/Italy)

La grande vadrouille/Don't Look Now, We're Being Shot At (GB/France)

1967   Jules Verne's Rocket to the Moon
       Arabella/*Ragazza dell autostrada* (GB/Italy)
       The Perils of Pauline (US)
       A Guide for the Married Man (US)
       Arriva Dorellik (Italy/Spain)
       Top Crack (Italy)
       Don't Raise the Bridge, Lower the River
       Diabolik (Italy)
1968   How Sweet It Is! (US)
       Uno scacco tutto matto (Italy/Spain)
       Where Were You When the Lights Went Out? (US)
       Sette volte sette (Italy)
1969   Arthur! Arthur!
       2000 Years Later (US)
       Una su tredici (Italy)
       Monte Carlo or Bust (US/Italy/France)
1970   *Le Mur de l'Atlantique* (France)
1971   The Abominable Dr. Phibes
       The Cherry Picker
1972   *Gli eroi*/ The Heroes (Italy/France/Spain)
       Colpo grosso … grossissimo … anzi probabile (Italy/Spain)
       Dr. Phibes Rises Again
1973   The Vault of Horror
       Robin Hood (US; *voice only*)
1975   The Bawdy Adventures of Tom Jones
       Side By Side
       Spanish Fly (GB/Spain)
1976   The Last Remake of Beau Geste (US)
1977   The Hound of the Baskervilles
1978   Kingdom of Gifts (*voice only*)
1980   *Febbre a 40*/ Happy Birthday Harry (Italy/Germany)

Barry Evans (1944–97)

1967   **Here We Go Round the Mulberry Bush**
1969   Alfred the Great
1972   Die Screaming, Marianne
       Journey to Murder (US TVM)
1975   Adventures of a Taxi Driver
1976   Under the Doctor
1993   The Mystery of Edwin Drood

Peter Cook (1937–95)

1962   Tarzan Goes to India
1966   The Wrong Box
1967   **Bedazzled**
1968   A Dandy in Aspic
1969   The Bed Sitting Room
        Monte Carlo or Bust
1970   The Rise and Rise of Michael Rimmer
1972   The Adventures of Barry McKenzie
1975   Find the Lady (Canada)
1977   Pleasure at Her Majesty's (*concert film*)
        The Hound of the Baskervilles
1979   The Secret Policeman's Ball (*concert film*)
        Derek and Clive Get the Horn (*unreleased theatrically*)
1983   Yellowbeard
1984   Supergirl
1986   Whoops Apocalypse
1987   The Princess Bride (US)
1988   Without a Clue
        Jake's Journey (US TVM)
1989   Getting It Right
        Great Balls of Fire! (US)
1994   Black Beauty

Dudley Moore (1935–2002)

1966   The Wrong Box
1967   **Bedazzled** (*and composed score*)
        30 Is a Dangerous Age, Cynthia (*composed score*)
1969   Monte Carlo or Bust (US/Italy/France)
        The Bed Sitting Room
1972   Alice's Adventures in Wonderland
1977   The Hound of the Baskervilles (*and composed score*)
1978   **Foul Play** (US)
1979   **10** (US)
1980   Wholly Moses (US)
1981   **Arthur** (US)
1982   Six Weeks (US; *and composed score*)
1983   Lovesick (US)
        Romantic Comedy (US)
        Unfaithfully Yours (US)
1984   Best Defense (US)
        Micki and Maude (US)
1985   Santa Claus (US)
1987   Like Father Like Son (US)

1988   Arthur 2: On the Rocks (US)
        Milo and Otis (US; *voice only*)
1990   Crazy People (US)
1992   Blame it on the Bellboy
        Parallel Lives (US TVM)
1995   The Disappearance of Kevin Johnson (US)
        Weekend in the Country (US TVM)

Mary Ure (1933–75)

1955   Storm Over the Nile
1957   Wisdom's Way
1959   **Look Back in Anger**
1960   **Sons and Lovers**
1963   The Mind Benders
1964   The Luck of Ginger Coffey (GB/Canada)
1966   Custer of the West (US/Spain)
1969   Where Eagles Dare
1973   The Daughter, aka Reflection of Fear (US)

Vivien Merchant (1929–82)

1966   **Alfie**
1967   **Accident**
1969   Alfred the Great
1971   Under Milk Wood
1972   **Frenzy**
        The Offence
1973   **The Homecoming**
1974   The Maids
1976   The Man in the Iron Mask (TVM)

Jill Bennett (1931*–90)

1952   Moulin Rouge (US)
1954   Hell Below Zero
1956   Lust for Life (US)
        The Extra Day
1960   The Criminal
1961   The Anatomist
1965   The Skull
        The Nanny
1968   The Charge of the Light Brigade
        Inadmissible Evidence

1970   Julius Caesar
1972   I Want What I Want
1976   Full Circle (*aka* The Haunting of Julia) (UK/Canada)
1979   The Old Crowd (TVM)
1981   For Your Eyes Only
1982   Britannia Hospital
1986   Lady Jane
1988   Hawks
1990   The Sheltering Sky (UK/Italy)
       * *Some reports suggest that Ms Bennett's birth was actually 1927*

Ian Hendry (1931–84)

1958   Room at the Top
1960   Sink the Bismark! (*uncredited*)
       In the Nick
1962   **Live Now —Pay Later**
1963   This Is My Street
       Children of the Damned
       The Girl in the Headlines
1964   **The Beauty Jungle**
1965   The Hill
       Repulsion
1966   The Sandwich Man
1967   *Los Traidores de San Ángel* (Spain)
1968   Cry Wolf
       L'Étoile du sud/The Southern Star (France)
1969   Doppelganger (*aka* Journey to the Far Side of the Sun)
1971   **Get Carter**
1972   Tales from the Crypt
       The Jerusalem File
       Captain Kronos: Vampire Hunter
1973   **Theatre of Blood**
       Assassin
1974   The Internecine Project
1975   *Professione: reporter* (*aka* The Passenger) (Italy)
1976   Intimate Games
1978   Damien: Omen II (US; *uncredited*)
1979   The Bitch
1980   McVicar

David Rappaport (1951–90)

1979   Mysteries (Netherlands)
       Cuba

The Secret Policeman's Ball
1981   **Time Bandits**
1983   Sword of the Valiant
1984   Unfair Exchanges (TVM)
1985   The Bride
1989   Peter Gunn (US TVM)
        Luigi's Ladies (Australia)

Charlotte Coleman (1968–2001)

1989   Bearskin: An Urban Fairytale (GB/Portugal)
1990   Sweet Nothing
1992   Map of the Human Heart (GB/Australia/France/Canada)
1994   Four Weddings and a Funeral
1995   The Young Poisoner's Handbook
1996   Different for Girls
1998   The Revengers' Comedies (GB/France)
        The Man with Rain in His Shoes (GB/US/France/Germany/Spain)
1999   Beautiful People
        Faeries (*voice only*)
        Bodywork
2001   A Loving Act (*short*)

Sir Stanley Baker (1927–76)

1943   Undercover
1949   All Over the Town
1950   Your Witness
1951   Lilli Marlene
        The Rossiter Case
        Cloudburst
        Captain Horatio Hornblower R.N.
        Home to Danger
1952   Whispering Smith Hits London
1953   **The Cruel Sea**
        The Red Beret
1954   Knights of the Round Table
        The Tell-Tale Heart
        Hell Below Zero
        The Good Die Young
        Beautiful Stranger
1955   Richard III
1956   Helen of Troy (US)
        Alexander the Great (US)
        A Child in the House

A Hill in Korea
Checkpoint
1957 **Hell Drivers**
Campbell's Kingdom
1958 Violent Playground
Sea Fury
1959 The Angry Hills
Blind Date
Jet Storm
Yesterday's Enemy
1960 **Hell is a City**
The Criminal
The Guns of Navarone
1961 Sodom and Gomorrah (France/Italy)
1962 Eve
A Prize of Arms
In the French Style
The Man Who Finally Died
1964 **Zulu** (*also co-produced*)
1965 Dingaka
One of Them is Named Brett (*documentary; as narrator*)
Sands of the Kalahari (*also co-produced*)
1967 **Accident**
Robbery (*also co-produced*)
1968 *La ragazza con la pistola* (*aka* The Girl with the Pistol) (Italy)
1969 Where's Jack? (*also produced*)
1970 The Last Grenade
The Games
Perfect Friday
1971 *Una lucertola con la pelle di donna* (*aka* A Lizard in Woman's
Skin) (France/Spain/Italy)
Popsy Pop (*aka* The Butterfly Affair; The 21 Carat Snatch)
(France/Italy)
1972 Innocent Bystanders
1975 Zorro (France/Italy)
Pepita Jiménez (*aka* Bride to Be) (Spain)
Orzowei, il figlio della savana (Italy TVM)

References

Articles

Peter Gillman, "Carol: A Candle in the Wind", *Sunday Times Magazine*, August 2, 1992 (Carol White)

Cal McCrystal, "Exit, With Tears", *The Independent on Sunday*, October 21, 1990 (Jill Bennett)

Denis Meikle, "Interview with the Werewolf", *The Little Shoppe of Horrors No. 15 (Journal of Classic British Horror Films)* (Oliver Reed)

Anthony Page, "Inadmissible Epitaph", *The Guardian*, June 6, 1992 (Jill Bennett)

Ian Parker, "A Short Life", *The Independent on Sunday*, May 4, 1991 (David Rappaport)

Barbara Paskin, "I'm Not Waiting To Die", *The Times*, October 20, 1999 (Dudley Moore)

Books

Richard Beckinsale, *With Love*, Frederick Muller Ltd 1980

Jill Bennett, *Godfrey — A Special Time Remembered*, Coronet 1985

Michael Billington, *The Life and Work of Harold Pinter*, Faber & Faber 1996

Humphrey Carpenter, *That Was Satire That Was*, Victor Gollancz 2002

Paul Donnelly, *Fade to Black: A Book of Movie Obituaries*, Omnibus Press 2000

Diana Dors, *Dors by Diana*, Macdonald Futura 1981

John French, *Robert Shaw — The Price of Success*, Nick Hern Books 1993

Cliff Goodwin, *Evil Spirits: The Life of Oliver Reed*, Virgin 2000

Leslie Halliwell, *Halliwell's Film Guide*, Grafton Books 1989

Freddie Hancock and David Nathan, *Hancock*, BBC Books 1986

Edward Joffe, *Hancock's Last Stand*, Methuen 1999

Roger Lewis, *Charles Hawtrey 1914–1988: The Man Who Was Private Widdle*, Faber & Faber 2001

Roger Lewis, *The Life and Death of Peter Sellers*, Arrow 1994

Mark Lewisohn, *Funny, Peculiar — The True Story of Benny Hill*, Sidgwick & Jackson 2002

Mark Lewisohn, *The Radio Times Guide to TV Comedy*, BBC Books 1998

David McGillivray, *Doing Rude Things*, Sun Tavern Fields 1992

Mary Millington and David Weldon, *The Amazing Mary Millington*, Futura 1979

John Osborne, *Almost A Gentleman — An Autobiography Vol II: 1955–66*, Faber & Faber 1992

Barbara Paskin, *Dudley Moore: The Authorized Biography*, Sidgwick & Jackson 1997

John Pym (ed.), *The Time Out Film Guide*, Penguin 2001

Robert Ross, *The Carry On Companion*, BT Batsford 1996

Robert Ross, *The Complete Terry-Thomas*, Reynolds & Hearn 2002

Michael Sellers, *PS — I Love You*, Collins 1981

Simon Sheridan, *Come Play With Me: The Life and Films of Mary Millington*, FAB Press 1999

Ed Sikov, *Mr Strangelove — A Biography of Peter Sellers*, Sidgwick & Jackson 2002

Anthony Storey, *Stanley Baker: Portrait of an Actor*, W.H. Allen 1977

Terry-Thomas (with Terry Baum), *Terry-Thomas Tells Tales*, Robson Books 1990

Harry Thompson, *Peter Cook — A Biography*, Hodder and Stoughton 1996

Alexander Walker (ed.), *No Bells on Sunday: The Journals of Rachel Roberts*, Sphere Books 1984

Alexander Walker, *Peter Sellers: The Authorised Biography*, Weidenfeld & Nicholson 1981

Carol White (with Clifford Thurlow), *Carol Comes Home*, New English Library 1982

Damon Wise, *Come By Sunday: The Fabulous, Ruined Life of Diana Dors*, Sidgwick & Jackson 1998

Index

'10' (1979) 90, 94, 99

Abominable Dr. Phibes, The (1971) 81
Accident (1967) 112, 135
Adventures of a Taxi Driver (1976) 86, 89
Adventures of Bullwhip Griffin, The (1965) 49
Ad Nauseam (album) 94
After Dark (TV) 24
Alfie (1966) 111
Alice's Adventures in Wonderland (1972) 61
Alpha Beta (stage) 18
Amazing Mr. Blunden, The (1972) 36, 58
Amorous Milkman, The (1974) 37
Anderson, Lindsay 16, 116
Andrews, Julie 56, 84
Ant, Adam 38
Antonioni, Michelangelo 123
Apted, Michael 9
Arnold, Mike 13, 14
Arthur (1981) 95, 97
Arthur 2 (1988) 99
Ashcroft, Peggy 112
Askwith, Robin 85, 88
Aspel and Company (TV) 24
Assassin (1973) 123
Austin, Jeremy 130
Avengers, The (TV) 120

Bach, Steven 64
Baker, Kenny 125
Baker, Sir Stanley 115, 133–137, 152
Bakewell, Joan 111
Barnard, Christiaan 58
Baron, David 110. See also Pinter, Harold
Bass, Alfie 41
Bates, Alan 26
Baum, Terry 81, 82, 84
Beals, Jennifer 127
Beatty, Warren 13, 98
Beat Girl (1960) 10
Beauty Jungle, The (1964) 121
Beckinsale, Richard 7, 8, 53–56, 144
Beckinsale, Samantha 55
Beckinsale, Kate 55
Bedazzled (1967) 90, 91
Bedtime for Rosie (1974) 37
Bed Sitting Room, The (1969) 90
Beerbohm Tree, Sir Henry 25
Behind the Fridge (stage) 92
Being There (1979) 62, 63, 64
Bennett, Alan 19, 116
Bennett, Jill 114–120, 150

Benny Hill's World (TV) 77
Benny Hill Show, The (TV) 72, 77
Bernsen, Corbin 125
Bertolucci, Bernardo 116
Best, George 28, 68
Best Defense (1984) 99
Beyond the Fringe (stage) 90
Billington, Michael 110, 111, 113
Birthday Party, The (stage) 110
Bisset, Jacqueline 11
Bitch, The (1979) 124
Blackman, Honor 120
Blackpool Show, The (stage) 50
Blind Date (1959) 133, 135
Blockhouse, The (1974) 56
Bloody Kids (1979) 54, 55
Bloomers (TV) 54, 55
Bobo, The (1967) 56
Bogarde, Dirk 135
Bough, Frank 83
Bradley, David 54
Bricusse, Leslie 23
Bride, The (1985) 127
Britannia Hospital (1982) 116
Brookside (TV) 124
Brown, Janet 83
Bull, Clive 95
Burke, Paul 11, 12, 13
Burnt Offerings (1976) 27
Burton, Richard 18, 33, 106, 133, 134

Caan, James 12
Cagney and Lacey (TV) 127
Caine, Michael 27,122
Campbell, Gavin 42
Campbell, Ken 125
Can We Talk? (TV) 95
Cardiff, Jack 105
Caretaker, The (1960) 110
Caretaker, The (stage) 111
Carpenter, Humphrey 96
Carry On (film series) 66, 67, 68, 69, 70, 71,
          83, 93. See also specific Carry On
          film titles
Carry On Abroad (1972) 68
Carry On Behind (1975) 69
Carry On Christmas (TV) 69
Carry On Dick (1974) 69
Carry On Emmanuelle (1978) 69
Carry On England (1976) 69
Carry On Girls (1973) 69
Carry on Teacher (1959) 10

Casino Royale (1967) 56, 121
Castaway (1986) 31
Castle, Roy 83
Cathy Come Home (1966) 10, 11
Chaplin, Charles 48
Charge of the Light Brigade, The (1968) 115
Charles, Prince 104
Charles, Ray 17
Charlie Chan and the Curse of the Dragon
    Queen (1981) 20, 21
Chase, Chevy 19, 94, 99
Chemin de Fer (stage) 19
Chitty Chitty Bang Bang (1968) 76
Christie, Agatha 110
Christie, Julie 13
Christopher, Sybil 22
Class of Miss McMichael, The (1978) 27
Cleese, John 96, 126
Cleopatra (1963) 134
Clive Anderson Talks Back (TV) 96, 97
Clive Bull Show (radio) 95
Coleman, Charlotte 129–132, 152
Collins, Joan 14
Collins, John 50
Come Again (album) 94
Come Play With Me (1977) 41, 42
Condorman (1981) 27
Confessions of … (film series) 87
Confessions from the David Galaxy Affair
    (1979) 37, 43
Connery, Sean 26, 27, 112, 121, 126, 127
Cook, Judy 95
Cook, Peter 90–97, 99, 101, 92, 149
Cook, Wendy 92
Corbett, Harry H 42
Cover Girl Killer (1959) 42
Coward, Noel 133
Crazy People (1990) 99
Criminal, The (1960) 115, 135
Crompton, Richmal 38
Curse of the Werewolf (1961) 25
Curtis, Richard 131
Curtis, Tony 56
Cushing, Peter 127
Custer of the West (1966) 106
Cutthroat Island (1995) 31

Daddy's Girls (TV) 101
Daddy's Gone A-Hunting (1969) 11
Dallas (TV) 127
Damien: Omen II (1978) 124
Dance of Death (stage) 116
Danger — Marmalade at Work (TV) 130
Darby O' Gill and the Little People (1958) 122
Daryl, Jacqui 26
Daughter, The (1973) 107
Davies, John Howard 72, 73, 75
Davies, Windsor 42
Davis, Geena 31

Dawson, Richard "Dickie" 33, 34
Day, Doris 80
Day the Earth Caught Fire, The (1962) 122
Debussy Film, The (TV) 26
Deep End (1970) 36
Deep Throat (1972) 41
Delaney, Shelagh 114
Deneuve, Catherine 121
Derek and Clive (Live) (album) 93
Des O' Connor Tonight (TV) 77
Devils, The (1971) 26, 27
Diamonds (1975) 108
Die Screaming Marianne (1972) 86
Diff'rent Strokes (TV) 13
Different for Girls (1996) 131
Doctor at Large (TV) 86
Doctor in the House (TV) 86
Doctor Who (TV) 130
Doppelganger (1969) 121
Dors, Diana 32–39, 142
Douglas, Jack 83, 84
Douglas, Melvyn 62
Dr. Dolittle (1967) 18
Dr. Phibes Rises Again (1972) 81
Dr Strangelove (1963) 61
Dulcima (1971) 12
Dumb Waiter, The (1959) 110
Dunn, Nell 14
Duvall, Shelley 126
Dynasty (TV) 127

EastEnders (TV) 84, 89
Easton, Sheena 87
Eastwood, Clint 74, 106
Educating Marmalade (TV) 130
Edwards, Blake 56, 60, 94, 99
Edwards, Glynn 38, 42
Electric Blue (film series) 73
Elton, Ben 75
Emmanuelle (1974) 41, 45
Emmanuelle in Soho (1981) 46
Endfield, Cy 134, 135
Enfield, Harry 96
English, Louise 78
Entertainer, The (1960) 114
Entertainer, The (stage) 114
Epitaph for George Dillon (stage) 114
Evans, Barry 84–90, 148
Evans, Lee 31
Eve (1962) 133
Exorcism, The (stage) 108, 109
Eyre, Richard 118

Febbre a 40 (1980). See Happy Birthday
    Harry
Feldman, Marty 81
Fiendish Plot of Dr Fu Manchu, The (1980)
    61, 63
Finney, Albert 16, 18, 33

Flea in Her Ear, A (1968) 17
Flynt, Larry 40
Fonda, Henry 98
Ford, Stephen 29
For Maddie With Love (TV) 124
For Your Eyes Only (1981) 116
Foul Play (1978) 19, 94, 99
Four Musketeers, The (1974) 26
Four Weddings and a Funeral (1994) 131
Fraser, Lady Antonia 113
Frears, Stephen 54
Freddie and Max (TV) 131
Frederick, Lynne 58, 59, 60, 63, 64, 65
French, John 107
Frenzy (1972) 112
From Russia with Love (1963) 106
Frost, David 65, 91
Fruchter, Rena 103, 104
Fugard, Athol 20
Full Circle (1977) 116
Funny Bones (1995) 31
Funny Peculiar (stage) 54

Galton, Ray 48, 49, 50
Get Carter (1970) 122
Ghost in the Noonday Sun (1973) 56
Gielgud, Sir John 126
Gilchrist, Roderick 132
Gilliam, Terry 126
Gilliatt, Penelope 115
Gillman, Peter 13, 15
Gladiator (2000) 31
Good Evening (stage) 92. *See also* Behind
    the Fridge
Graceless Go I (1974) 137
Grade, Sir Lew 56
Graham, 'Leapy' Lee 34
Grant, Hugh 131
Grasshopper, The (1969) 11
Gregory's Girl 85
Guare, John 116
Guest, Val 121

Hall, Peter 112, 126
Hall, Willis 115
Hamilton, Dennis 32, 33, 34
Hamlet (stage) 116
Hamlin, Harry 125
Hancock, Freddie 50
Hancock, Tony 3, 7, 48–53, 143
Hancock's (TV) 49, 50
Handl, Irene 41
Hannibal Brooks (1968) 26
Hannie Caulder (1971) 36
Happy Birthday Harry (1980) 81
Harlin, Renny 31
Harris, Richard 33
Harrison, Rex 15, 16, 17, 18, 19, 23
Harty, Russell 18

Have I Got News For You (TV) 97
Hawn, Goldie 19, 94
Hawtrey, Charles 66–72,145
Heaven's Gate (1980) 64
Hedda Gabler (stage) 115
Hell Below Zero (1954) 115
Hell Drivers (1957) 134
Hendry, Ian 120–125, 151
Here We Go Round the Mulberry Bush (1967)
    85
Hickox, Douglas 26
Hill, Benny 7, 48, 72–78, 121, 127, 141, 146,
    147
Hill, The (1965) 121
Hill Street Blues (TV) 127
Hislop, Ian 97
Hitchcock, Alfred 112
Hodges, Mike 122
Hoffman (1969) 56
Holmes, Richard 84
Homecoming, The (1965) 111
Homecoming, The (1973) 112
Hooperman (TV) 127
Hope-Hawkins, Richard 83
Hostage Tower, The (1980) 19
Hothouse, The (1959) 110
Hound of the Baskervilles, The (1977) 81, 93
Howard, Trevor 127
Howarth, Donald 34
Howerd, Frankie 78
How Do You Want Me? (TV) 131, 132
How Green Was My Valley (1976) 137
Huston, John 115

I'll Never Forget What's'isname (1967) 10,
    11, 25
I'm All Right Jack (1959) 61
Idiot Weekly, Price 2d, The (TV) 56
Illuminatus! (stage) 126
Inadmissible Evidence (1968) 115
Inadmissible Evidence (stage) 114
Informer, The (TV) 121
Innocent Bystanders (1972) 137
Inquisitor, The (TV) 34
Intimate Games (1976) 124
Italian Job, The (1969) 76, 137

Jackson, Michael 77
Jacques, Hattie 67, 69
James, Sid 48, 69
Jaws (1975) 27, 109
Jet Storm (1959) 134
Joffe, Edward 51, 52
Jokers, The (1966) 25
Jones, Tom 56
Julius Caesar (1970) 115

Keep It Up Downstairs (1976) 37
Kendall, Kay 16

King, Mike 10, 11, 13
King, Steve 13,15
Kirkland, Dennis 72, 73, 75, 76, 77, 78
Korda, Alexander 105
Kosinki, Jerzy 62
Kristel, Sylvia 41
Kubrick, Stanley 61

Lake, Alan 32, 33, 34, 36, 37, 38
Lancaster, Burt 98
Landau, Ely 112
Landis, Carole 17
Landscape (1969) 112
Last Days of Disco, The (1998) 55
Last Remake of Beau Geste, The (1976) 81
Last Summer (1976) 54
Late Night with David Letterman (TV) 24
Laurel, Stan 48
Layton, George 88
Lazenby, George 27
LA Law (TV) 125,127
Lean, David 32
Leigh, Vivien 34,110
Lemmon, Jack 74,80,84
Lerner, Dr Stuart 13
Lesson from Aloes, A (stage) 20,21
Lester, Mark 30
Letterman, David 24
Levin, Irv 11
Lewin, David 63
Lewis, Roger 59,66,70
Lewisohn, Mark 74,77
Le Mesurier, Joan 51
Life in Pieces, A (TV) 97
Like Father, Like Son (1987) 99
Linda (1960) 10
Live Now, Pay Later (1962) 120
Loach, Ken 10,11
Loe, Judy 54
Lolita (1962) 61
Loneliness of the Long Distance Runner, The
     (1962) 114
Long, Stanley 86
Look Back in Anger (1959) 105,114
Look Back in Anger (stage) 105,114
Losey, Joseph 112,115,134,135
Lotus Eaters, The (TV) 122,123
Lovelace, Linda 41
Lover, The (1962) 111
Lover, The (stage) 111
Lovers, The (TV) 53
Lovesick 98
Love for Love (stage) 108
Love Thy Neighbour (TV) 87
Luard, Nicholas 96
Lucas, George 125
Luck of Ginger Coffey, The (1964) 106
Lumet, Sidney 19,112,121
Lust for Life (1956) 115

Lynch, David 29

Maclaine, Shirley 62
Macnee, Patrick 120
Made (1972) 13
Mann, Roderick 60
Marks, Harrison 42
Marmalade Atkins in Space (TV) 130
Martin, Dean 28
Maxted, Mary 39. See also Millington, Mary
McCowan, Alec 112
McCrystal, Cal 117, 119
McVicar (1980) 124
Meikle, Denis 29, 30
Merchant, Vivien 109–114, 135, 150
Merton, Paul 97
Me and My Girl (stage) 78
Michell, Keith 36
Miller, 'Randy' Mandy 46
Milligan, Spike 56, 61, 65, 66, 126
Millington, Doreen 40
Millington, Mary 39–48, 143
Mills, John 12, 133
Mind Your Language (TV) 85, 87
Minnelli, Liza 98, 102
Minnelli, Vincente 115
Mirisch, Walter 60
Mirror Has Two Faces, The (1996) 101
Miss Borehole (1970) 39
Monkhouse, Bob 83
Monte Carlo or Bust (1969) 90
Moody, Ron 31
Moon, Keith 28
Moore, Dudley 7, 48, 84, 90, 91, 92, 93, 95,
     96, 97–105, 149
Moore, Roger 56
More, Kenneth 133
Morrissey, Paul 93
Moses, Albert 87
Moulder-Brown, John 36
Moulin Rouge (1952) 115
Munro, Janet 122
Murder by Death (1976) 61
Murder on the Orient Express (1974) 19
My Fair Lady (1964) 17, 18
My Fair Lady (stage) 23

Naked Truth, The (1957) 61
Nanny, The (1965) 115
Neil, Christopher 87
Never Let Go (1960) 10
Newman, Paul 98
Nicholson, Jack 123
Niven, David 28
Noah (stage) 50
Not Only… But Also (TV) 90, 91
No Blade of Grass (1970) 58
Nutcracker (1982) 14

O'Brien, Edna 111
O' Sullivan, Richard 88
O' Toole, Peter 33
Oedipus (stage) 36
Offence, The (1972) 112
Old Crowd, The (1979) 116
Old Crowd, The (TV) 19
Old Times (stage) 107, 112
Oliver! (1968) 26, 30
Oliver Twist (1948) 32
Olivier, Laurence 34, 115
Omnibus (TV) 77, 103
Only Two Can Play (1962) 61
Optimists of Nine Elms, The (1973) 61
Oranges Are Not the Only Fruit (1989) 131
Osborne, John 105, 106, 107, 114, 115, 116, 117, 118, 119, 122

Page, Anthony 115, 116
Parsons, Jane 28
Parting Shots (1998) 31
Party, The (1968) 61
Paskin, Barbara 102, 103
Passenger, The (1975) 123
Patriot For Me, A (stage) 115
Pearl Harbor (2001) 55
Perfect Friday (1970) 136
Pertwee, Jon 130
Peter Cook Talks Balls (1994) 96
Phase IV (1973) 58
Phillips, Leslie 81
Pink Panther, The (1963) 61
Pink Panther (TV) 61
Pink Panther Strikes Again, The (1976) 57, 59
Pinter, Harold 107, 110, 111, 112, 113, 114, 135
Plank, The (TV) 70
Platonov (stage) 16
Playbirds, The (1978) 42
Polanski, Roman 121
Poor Cow (1967) 10, 13
Porridge (1979) 54
Porridge (TV) 53
Porter, Nyree Dawn 124
Price, Vincent 36, 123
Prince, Reg 29
Prince and the Pauper, The (1977) 27
Prisoner of Zenda, The (1979) 60
Prize of Arms, A (1962) 133
Pryce, Jonathan 116
Punch and Judy Man, The (1962) 49
Purnell, Tony 78, 79, 80

Q9 (TV) 126
Queenie's Castle (TV) 34, 36

Ramirez, Darren 19, 21, 22
Randolph Hearst, William 40
Rappaport, David 125–129, 151

Rattigan, Sir Terence 116
Really Wild Animals (TV) 102
Rebel, The (1960) 48
Redgrave, Michael 133
Red Saturday (1979) 54. *See also* Bloody Kids
Reed, Josephine 30
Reed, Oliver 7, 13, 23–32, 139
Reed, Sir Carol 25, 26
Reflection of Fear (1973). *See* Daughter, The
Repulsion (1965) 121
Return of the Pink Panther, The (1975) 56, 57, 59
Revenge of the Pink Panther (1978) 59, 60
Reynolds, Burt 74
Richardson, Ralph 126
Richardson, Tony 114
Richmond, Fiona 39
Rise and Rise of Michael Rimmer, The (1970) 91
Rising Damp (TV) 53, 54
Rivers, Joan 95
Robbins, Sue 14
Roberts, Rachel 7, 15–23, 116, 139
Rogers, Peter 68, 69, 71
Romance of the Pink Panther, The (unmade) 64
Romantic Comedy (1983) 98
Room 101 (TV) 97
Rooney, Mickey 84
Rossiter, Leonard 53
Rothschild, Nicole 99, 101, 103
Russell, Ken 26

Sandford, Jeremy 11
Sands of the Kalahari (1965) 134
Sandwich Man, The (1966) 121
Santa Claus (1985) 99
Saturday Night and Sunday Morning (1960) 15, 114
Saunders, James 54
Scent of Mystery 33
Schizo (1976) 59
Schlesinger, John 19
Schneider, Maria 123
Schoch, Thomas 116, 117
Scofield, Paul 105
Scott, Ridley 31
Sea Fury (1958) 134
Secombe, Harry 65
Segal, George 94, 99, 101
Sellers, Michael 63, 65
Sellers, Peter 7, 10, 27, 48, 56–66, 80, 98, 144
Separate Tables (stage) 116
Shaw, Robert 27, 105, 106, 107, 108, 109
Sheltering Sky, The (1990) 116
Shot in the Dark, A (1964) 56, 61
Show Called Fred, A (TV) 56

Sillitoe, Alan 114
Simpson, Alan 48, 49, 50
Sinatra, Frank 12
Sitting Target (1972) 26
Six Weeks (1982) 98
Six Wives of Henry VIII, The (1972) 58
Skolimowski, Jerzy 36
Soft Beds, Hard Battles (1973) 56
Some Call It Loving (1973) 13
Sons and Lovers (1960) 105,107
Son of Fred (TV) 56
Southern Star, The (1969) 121
Spanish Fly (1975) 81
Squeeze, The (1977) 9,13
Staircase (1968) 18
Star Trek: The Next Generation (TV) 129
Star Wars 125
Steaming (1984) 38
Steaming (stage) 14
Sting 127
Sting, The (1973) 27,107
Storm Over the Nile (1955) 105
Streisand, Barbra 101
Strindberg, August 116
Sullivan, David 40,42,43
Supergirl (1984) 95
Supergran (TV) 71
Swedish Wildcats (1974) 37
Swiss Family Robinson (1960) 122
Sword of the Valiant (1983) 127
Sykes, Eric 70
Symington, Martin 89
System, The (1964) 25

T-T. See Terry-Thomas
Taffner, Don 77
Taste of Honey, A (1961) 114
Tearle, Sir Godfrey 115,119,120
Terry-Thomas 48,78–84,147
That's Life (TV) 42
Theatre of Blood (1973) 36,123
There's A Girl in My Soup (1970) 56
This is Your Life (TV) 30
This Sporting Life (1963) 16
Thomas, Gerald 68,69,71
Thompson, Harry 92,95
Thompson, J Lee 33
Thomson, Ada 109, 110. See also Merchant,
    Vivien
Three Months Gone (stage) 34
Three Musketeers, The (1973) 26
Thurlow, Clifford 13,14
Time Bandits (1981) 125,126,127
Time Present (stage) 115
Time Remembered (stage) 105
Tinker, Jack 113,114
Tiswas (TV) 126
Todd, Barbara Euphan 130
Tommy (1975) 26

Tom Jones (1963) 114
Tony Randall Show, The (TV) 19
Trail of the Pink Panther (1982) 60,65
Two of Us, The (TV) 95

Under the Doctor (1976) 87
Unfaithfully Yours (1984) 98
Unger, Barry 65
Up the Junction (TV) 11
Ure, Mary 105–109, 150
Ustinov, Peter 20,21

Vampire Circus (1972) 58
Vault of Horror (1973) 81
Venom (1981) 27
Ventham, Wanda 123
Visit, The (stage) 19
Volpone (stage) 126
Voyage of the Damned (1976) 58

Waiters, The (1971) 76
Walker, Alexander 22,62
Walker, Peter 59,86
Walters, Thorley 83
Warhol, Andy 93
Warner, David 126
Weld, Tuesday 92,103
West of Suez (stage) 115
What's New Pussycat? (1965) 61
Where Do I Sit? (TV) 92
Where Eagles Dare (1969) 106,107
White, Carol 9–15, 138
Whitehouse, Mary 40
Whoops Apocalypse (1986) 95
Whose Line Is It Anyway? (TV) 97
Why Bother? (radio) 97
Wilcox, Paula 53
Wilde, Cornel 58
Williams, Kenneth 66,67,69,71
Williamson, Shaun 84
Wilson, Harold 137
Windsor, Barbara 68,83
Winner, Michael 10, 25, 28, 31
Wise, Damon 38
Without a Clue (1988) 95
Wizard, The (TV) 127
Wolfitt, Sir Donald 110
Women in Love (1969) 11, 26, 27
Worzel Gummidge (TV) 130, 131

Yanks (1979) 19
Yield to the Night (1956) 33, 34
Young Ones, The (TV) 130
Young Poisoner's Handbook, The (1995) 131

Zulu (1964) 134, 137